# A Parent's Guide to
# YOUTH SOCCER

A publication of Leisure Press
597 Fifth Ave., New York, New York 10017

ISBN 0-88011-201-8
Library of Congress No. 83-80731


Cover photograph by Sab Frinzi

Cover Design: Tanya Edgar
Typesetting and Pasteup: H&C Custom Publishing Co., Inc., Emeryville, CA


Text photos credited as noted in the text
except those listed below:
Page 10A: Joe Van Woerden
12A: Stanford University Athletic Dept.
10: Bill Clare
12: Stanford University Athletic Dept.
72: J. J. O'Malley (**The Pocono Record**)
78: Wayne Glusker
104: Phil Digginger

# A Parent's Guide to
# YOUTH SOCCER

## Carolyn J. Mullins

**LEISURE PRESS**

NEW YORK

*For Jorge, who taught;*

*Rob, who learned;*

*And the Bloomington Pampas and their parents*

# CONTENTS

*Continued*

# PREFACE

In America, the parents of most young soccer players find themselves in a unique situation. Unlike most games and sports, which maintain themselves in part by being passed from parent to child, American soccer is growing by being passed from child to parent!

This book is for the parents of soccer players everywhere. Many of you didn't play the sport as children, so this book tells what equipment to get and how to choose it, how to help your child develop basic soccer skills, how to protect his or her physical and mental health, and how to support the soccer coach's work. To help you understand the coach's role in your child's life, the book explains both recreational and competitive soccer.

To help you understand the game, I've included a description of the field, lists of resources, and a discussion of rules and officials. Because soccer is new or not organized in many communities, an appendix describes the major national soccer programs. Because Americans are a people on the go, frequently moving from an area with youth soccer to one without, a second appendix tells how to start a team and organize a youth program.

The spirit of soccer is infectious. Properly played, soccer has a musical rhythm and grace all its own, although not unlike that of well-played man-to-man basketball. It is also innately nonviolent, even though players frequently make contact with each other.

The infection is incurable. Soon after our son Rob started playing, we hardly ever saw him without a soccer ball on his toe, and one evening we found him fast asleep with his soccer ball cradled in his arms.

To my surprise, I found myself saving time to watch not only Rob's games but also his practices. I, who love nothing better than a quiet hour with the word processor, discovered that some of my best ideas were being born on the grassy hill above my son's soccer field. The next thing I knew, Nick, my husband, and I had become the team's managers. Nick and our other son had become licensed referees. By 1980, Nick had joined his own recreational team.

For all families we wish the joys that soccer has brought our family. It is one of the few activities that we all do together. Furthermore, the discipline and commitment Rob has learned on a competitive team have carried over to other areas of his life, and he's learned how to make choices between soccer and other valued activities. These traits will serve him well for the rest of his life. We wish the same benefits for other players.

For reading an earlier draft of this book and making valuable suggestions on how to improve it, I am grateful to Jorge Oclander, Rob's Argentinian coach, who commented on the chapters and explained the fine points of soccer; to Paul Harris of Soccer for Americans, co-author of *Fair or Foul* and author of *So You'd Like to Know More about Soccer!* and many other books, for his detailed and thoughtful comments and general encouragement for the project; and to Hubert Vogelsinger, player, coach, and director of the Puma All-Star Soccer School, who contributed many fine pictures and critiqued the next-to-last draft of the book. Martha Oman read the final draft. Without the help of these experts, this book couldn't have achieved its current level of accuracy. (I am, of course, responsible for any remaining errors.)

Many people and organizations contributed pictures to illustrate the text. For this help I thank adidas USA inc.; John Beaulieu, Stretching Charts; Action & Leisure, Inc. (Patrick, Uhlsport); Indiana University Women's Soccer Club, Steve Parker, coach; National Collegiate Athletic Association; Soccer Sport Supply Co., Inc. (Doss, Soccer Sport); Sports & Leisure International, Inc. (Mikasa); Umbro Soccer Education Division; Hubert Vogelsinger, Puma All Star Soccer School; Union Jacks; and Jerry Yeagley, coach, Indiana University men's soccer and director, Indiana Soccer Camp. The pictures provided by Hubert Vogelsinger, including the cover picture, were taken by Sab Frinzi, Frinzi Studios, 661 Hartford Turnpike, Hamden, Connecticut 06471.

*Continued*

From time to time throughout this book, I mention the observations of various authorities. To avoid burdening the text with academic formalities, I don't give full bibliographic information in the text. Full bibliographic information is in the bibliography, alphabetized by author's last name.

This book is especially for Rob, who has been putting the best of himself into soccer since 1978, and for Jorge, who changed not only Rob's life but our whole family's when he became part of it.

It is also for Rob's teammates on the Bloomington Pampas and for their parents. Most of the players have doubled their size in the years I've been privileged to watch them grow; they are verging on adulthood. Their parents are dear friends with whom we've shared lots of laughter, cheers, tears, long trips, crowded motel rooms, and hard work. This team has two more years to play before college claims most of the players. I will miss the players and the soccer-filled weekends, but I'll miss the parents most of all.

Carolyn J. Mullins<br>
Bloomington, Indiana

# PART I:
# THE GAME

# A Game
# For Everyone

Games that resemble modern soccer have long been played in countries around the world. The histories of Greece, China, Japan, and Rome mention soccer-like games. In fourteenth century England, the game was banned due to fear of the great crowds that soccer matches drew, but soccer managed to survive. Today, much of the world still calls the game "football," "association football," or "soccer-football." These terms sometimes confuse Americans, who assume that the reference is to the American game of football. (Unlike soccer, though, American football is played as much with the hands as with the feet.)

The long-standing popularity of soccer is due in part to children's fascination with kicking and chasing balls — what Hubert Vogelsinger calls "the magic of the ball." In South America, my son's coach says, infants learn to "dribble" the ball with their feet almost before they can toddle. Soccer not only exploits the fascination with balls but adds the challenge of moving the ball totally without hands.

Soccer is also popular, Vogelsinger says, because it develops team and social skills. Furthermore people who play soccer find that it prepares them well to play many other sports.

And in fitness-conscious America, soccer attracts participants because it develops physical endurance, agility, and cardiovascular fitness and has a low rate of injury compared to most other sports.

When Rob started playing soccer, these virtues were readily apparent. He was fascinated not only by kicking but by moving the ball with his head, thigh, leg — anything but a hand or arm. Accurate passing to a teammate rapidly became a matter of pride to him, and he was constantly on the move, running from one end or side of the field to the other. The swift pace of the action involved him totally. Long before we understood much about the game, Nick and I knew that our son had lost his heart to a game designed for a ball with six-sided patches.

One joy of soccer is that any person, male or female, large or small, young or old, can play the game. The game itself depends on structure and team play. The important factors are skill and intelligence, not size. Indeed, one of Rob's teammates, a fullback, is a petite young lady who regularly outwits players twice her size. For spectators, the game offers continuous action with few, if any, time outs.

# The Sound of Music

My introduction to soccer was unlike anything else I'd encountered in my children's participation in sports. The first time I visited my son's practice field, I heard music coming from a small portable tape recorder on the soccer field! And dribbling a ball in time to the music were Rob and his teammates. I was startled. Many weeks later, though I noticed that the players who had been having trouble when I first saw them were working much more smoothly with teammates. A few minutes later the players lined up and began to "follow the leader" around the field; the leader snapped his fingers, clapped his hands, and slapped his thighs in ever-changing patterns that the other players had to copy. These actions, I learned later, were called "Brazilian warm-ups."

We'd already begun to suspect that the coach, Argentinian Jorge Oclander, was a highly unusual individual. One of the first stories we'd heard about him came from a father whose son had played for Jorge in Bloomington's recreational league. When Gus Nelson first saw Jorge, he was standing with several players who had arrived early. Balanced on one crutch, Jorge was using the other to demonstrate how he wanted the players to kick the ball. (At the time, Jorge was recovering from a bad automobile accident.) Not at all certain a man on crutches could manage a teamful of active boys, Gus stuck around to offer a hand. (He found no cause for concern.)

When I inquired about the music, Jorge explained that rhythm was essential to good soccer. "If all the players have the same internal rhythm," he said, "they move together better and pass and dribble better." The Brazilian warm-ups also contribute to the development of rhythm but were even more important for another reason. "Players have to work off each other's rhythm, so using a modified form of follow-the-leader gets them used to anticipating how a teammate moves. The act of imitating makes them 'take into' themselves a teammate's rhythm, and that also helps them pass more accurately on the field."

Jorge's next statement cleared up a mystery. On several prior occasions I'd asked Rob how practice had gone, only to be told, "Oh, we didn't practice, we just whistled and played some games with the ball. We had a great time."

"The music makes practice fun," Jorge continued. "The players learn everything I want them to, and they don't realize they're working. How else am I going to get them to practice the same move 50 times without getting bored or impatient or mad? How can you get mad when you're humming or whistling?" A very good question. How can you?

Jorge believes firmly that, "If it isn't elegant, it isn't soccer. The most important thing to teach a young player," Jorge continued, "is to be gentle and caring with the ball. Watch the Argentines in the 1978 World Cup. Player and ball are as one, moving rhythmically — that is beautiful soccer!" It is also highly effective. Most teams in our league play a long-passing style of soccer. Our team plays South American low, close-passing soccer. Rob learned early never to kick the ball unless he had someone in mind to receive it. "Don't kill the ball, love it!" Jorge often reminded the players. His basic idea was, "If you pass accurately and control the ball between passes, the other team won't get the ball often enough for long passes to do any damage." And, of course, if the opponents don't have the ball, they can't score.

The value of practicing with music was driven home recently after a game in which Rob (a left halfback) and Kahlil Stewart (the center halfback) had been passing to each other with perfect teamwork. When I commented admiringly, Rob responded, "Oh, that was easy, Mom; we were both humming 'Funkytown.'"

South American soccer depends on teamwork, and it took Jorge nearly two months to develop enough of it to win a game. He had warned us that the South American style took time to develop. Once mastered, though, it would be very difficult for opponents to handle. And indeed, in June 1979 our team, less than a year old, took second place in the state tournament. In June 1981 the team once again took second in the Under-14 state championship.

**Fig. 1.1** Indiana University soccer player (white uniform) has a "man on" him, trying to steal the ball. Photograph used by permission of Jerry Yeagley, Coach, Indiana University men's soccer team. In December 1982 IU's Soccer Hoosiers won the NCAA championship for the first time, beating Duke 2-1 in a marathon game that was tied 1-1 at the end of regulation time and then went through 2 15-minute overtime periods and nearly 40 additional minutes of sudden-death overtime before Greg (Thumper) Thompson finally scored on a direct kick after being fouled.

**Fig. 1.2** Indiana University's soccer player (white uniform) traps the ball inside his thigh while trying to protect it from the on-coming defender. Photograph used by permission of Indiana University men's soccer team.

This is not to say that all you need is a Latin coach who loves music and coaches on crutches. As a former goalie, Jorge knew goalkeeping and offense well, but he often needed "expert help on other skills, especially defense." His solution was to recruit specialists as consultants. He felt his greatest weakness as a teacher was in the defensive theories of the game. So, he asked Joe Kelly, assistant coach for Jerry Yeagley's Indiana University soccer team and a defensive specialist, to spend the two weeks before a state tournament working with the team for three hours each day. During the winter 1980 practices, Armando Betancourt, 1981 Hermann Award winner and a forward on Indiana University's team, worked with the team and frequently attended games.

"A coach, especially in youth divisions, can't try to gloss over his or her weaknesses," Jorge says, "because the players get *their* attitude toward learning from the coach. If I still work at learning, they will, too."

# The Kinds of Soccer

Like other sports in America, soccer is played both recreationally and competitively. Nearly all players start their careers in recreational soccer, and many stay with it for a lifetime. Highly skilled players often shift to competitive soccer.

Parents need to know which kind of soccer best suits each of their children. Recreational soccer is nearly always the right choice for young children (up to age 8 or 9). It is also the right choice for a child who simply enjoys kicking the ball around for fun or exercise.

Somewhere between the ages of 9 and 12, though, some highly skilled players begin to want something more challenging than recreational soccer. They still want to have fun with the game, but they also want more challenge. As they grow older, many decide that soccer is *their* game, and they want to play it to the exclusion of other sports.

Parents who prevent a qualified child from playing competitive soccer only frustrate the child. In addition, the very talented player who plays only for a recreational team may develop an overblown sense of his own importance.

Conversely, parents who push unqualified children into competitive play may kill their love for the game. More important, these children may develop a sense of inferiority from their failure to match their teammates' skill or their parents' expectations.

**Recreational Soccer**

**Recreational** soccer, the oldest form of the game, emphasizes participation and learning. Players are assigned to teams randomly, sometimes with a geographic bias to make transportation easy. Boys and girls often play together on the same teams. Games are with other local recreational teams. Coaches teach basic skills, play each player 50% of the time without regard to ability, and do not drop players once a team is formed. With most players, soccer is only one of several activities or sports and is not necessarily the players' top priority. Most of these players play soccer purely for fun and relaxation; unlike competitive players, they do not want to organize even a part of their lives around the game.

Recreational soccer sometimes occurs as a neighborhood pickup game and often occurs as a community-based activity sponsored by a local parks and recreational department, a local school, or a local association such as the Boys' Club, Girls' Club, YMCA, YWCA, and youth soccer associations. Local recreational programs often work as branches of national soccer organizations such as the United States Soccer Federation (USSF), American Youth Soccer Association (AYSO), and Soccer Association for Youth (SAY). (Appendix A contains information on these organizations.)

In these forms, soccer costs very little. The only essential equipment is a ball and a pair of shoes (called "cleats"), and many recreational players use sneakers in place of cleats. In addition, a team in formal competition needs some kind of uniform, even if only tee shirts in the same color. Again, many boys' recreational teams make do with "shirts and skins." Helpful, although not essential for recreational soccer, are several balls for practice, nets to hang on goalposts, and a line painter and paint.

**Competitive Soccer**

For a few highly skilled players, competitive soccer grows naturally out of recreational soccer. Soccer has become *their* sport, and they want to invest a great deal of their time in it.

The purpose of **competitive** soccer is to provide a structure within which highly skilled players can continue to develop their soccer skills through competition with top teams. Thus, players chosen on the basis of ability play against teams similarly chosen. The best teams play in league competition and in regional and national tournaments. Many of these players want to play soccer competitively in college and beyond. Playing time is determined by the coach, based on the needs of the team in each game. Important values are improving skills, learning teamwork, playing to potential, and fielding and playing against the best teams possible. Having fun, then, is only one of several important goals.

**Fig. 1.3** Defenders (black uniforms) close in on Indiana University ball carrier, trying to prevent a pass. Photograph used by permission of Indiana University Men's Association.

**Fig. 1.4** Under the watchful eye of the referee, Indiana University players (dark uniforms) move to take the ball away from their opponents (white uniforms). Picture used by permission of Indiana University Women's Soccer Club, Steve Parker, coach.

The United States Youth Soccer Association (USYSA; see Appendix A) has a formal competitive team program. Each player on a competitive team *must* have a player **pass** or **card** that signifies membership in the United States Soccer Federation (USSF). To receive a card each player must 1) fill out and sign a form, 2) obtain his or her parent's signature on the form, and 3) give to the team manager or club or association registrar the completed form, two recent photos or snapshots, and a copy of his or her birth certificate or other documentary proof of age. The manager or registrar submits these items to the state association, which registers the players with the USSF and returns a pass for each player to either the manager or an association registrar.

Competitive players are segregated by age. A youth soccer player's age for an entire year is established by his or her age on January 1. For example, Rob was 11 on January 1, 1979, so he was defined as "Under-12" from September 1, 1978, through August 31, 1979, even though he became 12 on March 17, 1979. On January 1, 1980, though, he was 12 and so had to move into Under-14 play as of September 1, 1979. States with new programs, like Indiana's, often group two birth years' worth of players in one age bracket. Areas that have large, well-established programs usually group by birth year. In such areas, players Rob's age usually play mainly with and against others born in 1967.

In addition to player registration, each team must file a **roster** each season that lists up to 18 players and records their signatures. Local, state, and national rules define a team year as running from September 1 through the following August 31.

As is the case with any sport played competitively, practices are mandatory. Soccer emphasizes the team. Individuals are important in relationship to the entire team, and individual skills are developed, evaluated, and applied according to the team's need.

To develop the necessary team qualities, each player must be able to 1) be responsible in all phases of the game, 2) concentrate on assignments, 3) accept criticism gracefully, 4) support teammates, 5) be a willing learner, 6) strive to have the team excel, and 7) play and practice to the highest potential. Not every soccer player can (or should attempt to) do these things, but most players on competitive teams accept these guidelines in some form.

Players and families need to recognize that even players who starred in a recreational league will not necessarily star, or even start, on a competitive team. Many players will start one game and not the next, depending on the strengths of the opposing team and the particular needs of their team.

Players in areas where competitive soccer is just developing may have responsibilities in addition to practices. For instance, many players need to help with funding and administration — lining fields, putting up nets, making telephone calls, and so forth. Many make excellent public representatives as they accompany adults on fund-raising visits and to club meetings to publicize their team's need for sponsors. My son and his teammates worked side by side with parents at a garage sale that netted more than $1000 for travel expenses.

Sponsors are important because competitive play costs money. In 1982 tournament entry fees ranged upwards from $75. Furthermore, while host teams often invite visitors to stay with their families, sometimes teams have to stay in a motel. Even with several players in the same room, the cost for a weekend trip can go as high as $50 per player. In addition, families who travel with the team have to pay their own expenses. Some families can't afford the trips for either themselves or their children.

**Select Team Soccer**

There are two kinds of select team soccer. One type occurs when several teams pool their best players to form a select team for tournament play. By definition, players on these select teams are not ordinarily teammates.

The second type, made possible by the USYSA's National Select Team Program, enables exceptionally talented players to further develop their skills. Each state association administers a state select team program that leads, ultimately, to trials to choose players for the National Select Team. Any player is eligible to participate within the specific age limits. In addition to the chance to try out for the National Select Team, players chosen for all-state teams play with those teams against all-state teams from other states. Up to 1980, the select team program operated only for boys aged Under-14 through Under-19, but the increased number of girl soccer players has inspired many states to begin similar programs for them.

# PART II:
# PLAYING
# THE GAME

# The Playing Field and Player Positions

The playing field has minimum dimensions of 50 x 100 yards and maximum dimensions of 100 x 130 yards (Law #1, Federation Internationale de Football Association). Figure 2.1 on the next page shows a picture of the soccer field with the various parts marked. Figure 2.2, following page, shows the outline of a field with offensive and defensive players marked on it.

## Field Markings

The **center line**, also known as the **halfway line**, divides the field into two halves for kickoffs and helps referees to call "offside" (explained in Chapter 5).

The **goal** lines, at each end of the field, are boundaries that determine whether a ball is in or out of play. The part of the line that is between the goal posts helps referees to determine a fair goal. (A goal is scored whenever the ball goes completely over the line, either in the air or on the ground, between the goalposts.) The goal line is considered part of the goal area. Thus, a ball that is on the line is in bounds, not out.

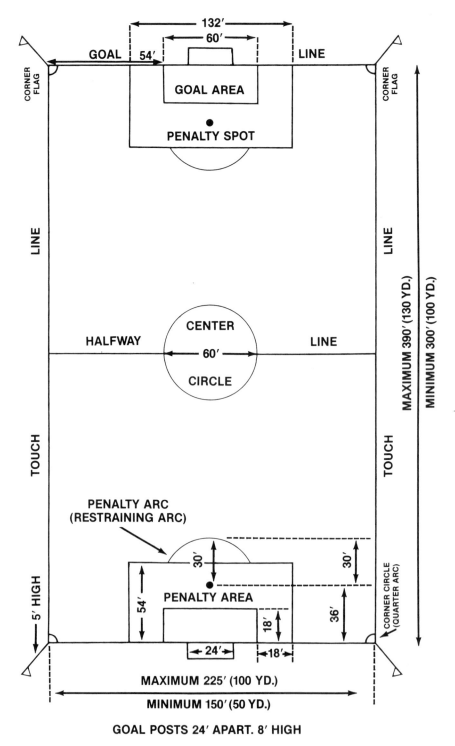

**Fig. 2.1** Diagram of field with parts marked. Notice that the length and width can vary.

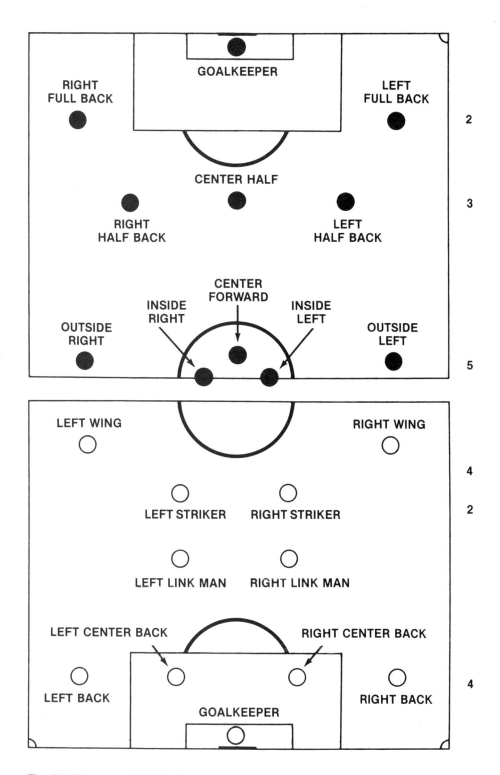

**Fig. 2.2** Diagram of field with positions marked. Notice that some positions are given several names.

The **side** or **touch** lines, like the goal lines, are boundaries that determine whether the ball is in or out of play. Also like the goal lines, the side lines are considered part of their areas. A ball that is on the line is judged to be in bounds. When a ball goes out of bounds, it is put into play by a throw-in from the spot where it went out.

The **goal area** marks the area within which members of the opposing team may fairly charge a goalkeeper who has possession of the ball. The goal area also helps referees to determine the accurate placement of goal kicks (explained in Chapter 5).

Within the **penalty area**, which includes the goal area, goalkeepers may use their hands on the ball. Furthermore, all kicks awarded to the defense must leave this area before they can be played by either team.

The **penalty spot** is the spot within the penalty area from which the offensive team takes "penalty kicks" (explained in Chapter 5).

The **restraining arc** or **penalty arc**, a crescent-shaped area at the edge of the penalty area, is meant to keep players at least 10 yards from the ball before the taking of a penalty kick.

The **corner circle** or **quarter arc** shows where to place the ball on "corner kicks" (explained in Chapter 5).

The **center circle** is the restraining area for all defensive players whenever the ball is kicked off.

# Player Positions

Each team starts the game with eleven players. One is the **goalkeeper** or **goalie**. (Sometimes you'll hear very young or very new soccer players refer to this person as the "goldie.") The goalie sometimes wears gloves and is required to wear a shirt that is a different color from all other shirts on the playing field. Goalkeepers can use their hands on the ball *as long as they are in the penalty area*. They are the only players on the field who may ever use their hands on the ball while it is in play. (All players may handle the ball when they are throwing the ball in from out of bounds; see Chapter 4.)

The **fullbacks** or **backs**, who are directly in front of the goalie, play primarily a defensive game. Their main duty is to keep the ball away from the goal area. A team may have from two to four fullbacks, depending on the formation the team is using. Naturally, the more players in the fullback position, the fewer are left for other positions. Often players act as fullbacks when the ball is close to their goal and move up to play offensively when their team is trying to score. Sometimes you'll hear a fullback referred to as a **sweeper** or **stopper**. In over-simplified terms, the reason for these names is that these backs have special responsibility for "stopping" balls and "sweeping" them from the goal area.

The **halfbacks** are sometimes called **linkmen** because they "link" a team's offense with its defense. They work hard on both offense and defense, helping to both form and stop attacks.

The **forwards**, often called **strikers** because their main task is to try to score goals, are usually quicker than the half- and fullbacks. The left and right forwards are often called **wings** or **wingers**. Some coaches call the center forward the **target** or **or target man.**

When children start playing soccer, they generally try all positions. Specialization later is determined by personal preference, individual strengths, and team needs.

Unlike American football, soccer teams are not divided into offensive and defensive specialists. In comparison to football coaches, soccer coaches seldom substitute players. Substitution is most common in recreational soccer in which each player is expected to play at least half the time. In competitive soccer, though, players often play the entire game (up to 90 minutes) with no substitute unless they are injured.

## Strategic Formations

This section explains some common formations very briefly. Some writers devote whole chapters and even whole books to one or a few formations. If you want to learn more, read Vogelsinger's *The Challenge of Soccer*, Morris' *The Soccer Tribe*, or any of the books for coaches listed in the bibliography.

In soccer, the various formations are important mainly as general concepts that shape a team's positions on offense and defense. They are usually not maintained rigidly. Nevertheless, you'll enjoy the game more if you recognize the strengths and weaknesses of popular formations. Figure 2.2 (top half, from goal to midline) shows the 2-3-5 offensive formation, which is popular for putting five players in likely scoring positions. The bottom half of the figure shows the 4-2-4 set-up, which balances primarily scoring players with primarily defending players and enables smooth shifts between offense and defense.

An offensive set-up with four fullbacks, three halfbacks, and three forwards adds strength to the midfield. An offense with four fullbacks, four halfbacks, and two forwards emphasizes speed in changing from offense to defense.

Not surprisingly, defensive set-ups are designed to counter the various offenses. For instance, a three-fullback defense is stronger than one with two fullbacks, but it still may not provide enough protection to cover a four-person forward line. Using four fullbacks solves that problem but creates others by taking one of those backs from the midfield. Emphasizing man-to-man **marking** (guarding) over defense of specific territory on the field can help solve that problem.

The difference between the two approaches is like the difference between man-to-man and zone defense in basketball.

Coaches choose one formation over another partly in response to the formation's innate strategic value and partly in response to the strengths of the team's personnel. Thus, an injury to certain players may cause a coach to change formations. For instance, if injury sidelines a team's only experienced goalkeeper, the coach might respond by changing to a formation with more fullbacks than he or she might ordinarily use.

If your child is very young (8 or younger), you probably won't see any consistent formations at all except, perhaps, one that looks rather like a football huddle. There's nothing strategic about the huddle — it's just that young children tend to gather around the ball and follow it in bunches rather than playing fixed positions.

# Equipment: Choosing and Caring for It

Parents of soccer players are often pleasantly surprised to find that soccer equipment costs less than equipment for many other sports. Indeed, some experts say that it costs less to equip an entire soccer team than to outfit one average American football player! This chapter tells what equipment players need and how to care for it.

## Balls

All soccer players need their own good soccer ball. *Don't* buy one of the toy soccer balls that has the black-and-white six-sided patches painted on. These balls don't hold up under serious soccer practice. Good balls, which should always be equipped with a valve for proper inflation, can be made of leather, polyurethane, or PVC (polyvinyl chloride), and may be nylon wound. It isn't necessary that the ball be hand-sewn. Choose a ball that carries the official approval of one of the major soccer organizations — FIFA (Federation Internationale de Football Association), ASL (American Soccer League), AYSO, USSF, or NASL (North American Soccer League).

Don't pump the ball too full of air, and dry it off when it gets wet during practice. With proper care, a ball will last two or three years.

Choose the proper size for your child. Size 3, the official size for Midget Leagues, is suitable for children aged 3 to 8 years. Size 4, slightly larger, is for children approximately 8 through 11 years. Size 5 is the regulation size for children 12 and older and for adults. Figure 3.1, Part A, shows balls in all three sizes. Balls in the other picture are size 5.

**Fig. 3.1-A** This picture shows balls in sizes 3, 4, and 5. Picture used with permission of Umbro Soccer Education Division.

**Fig. 3.1-B** These pictures show a variety of size 5 balls. Photographs of Doss and Soccer Sport balls used with permission of Soccer Sport Supply Company, Inc.

# Shoes

Soccer shoes, also called "cleats," come in many sizes, makes, and designs (see Figure 3.2). Good shoes are made of leather (full-grain, calf, or split), are lightweight, lined with a material that breathes, reinforced at the heel with leather or polyurethane, and equipped with an achilles tendon support that is padded for extra comfort and protection. The toecap should be soft and flexible but strong, with no exposed interior stitching to irritate the foot (check for stitching by putting your hand in the shoes and running your fingers around the toecap). The tongue should be padded, but not excessively, and should extend no more than a quarter of an inch above the top lacing. Some coaches want the laces to be long enough to lend support to both the ankle and the instep. In their view, if the laces are only long enough to wrap under the shoe, they are too short. Other coaches forbid wrapping of the lace on the ground that it hinders blood circulation in the foot and thus causes cramps.

The bottom of the shoes should have soft rubber molded studs — the more studs the better, because they cushion the foot. In general, especially for young children, avoid shoes with coated metal screw-in studs. The coating wears down and the studs must be replaced, which means your child has to remember to carry replacements with him. More important, the screw-in studs slip on hard surfaces and may cause knee injuries by not allowing proper rotation of the foot and leg. Similarly, the metal studs can be dangerous to opponents. Referees line up players before each game and check the studs on everyone's shoes. Players with metal showing aren't allowed to play.

The shoes should fit snugly, with the toes tight but not cramped. Because leather stretches, players often buy a half size smaller than

**Fig. 3.2** Soccer cleats come in various sizes, models, and designs. The combination of cleats and wedges on the sole of the Patrick Stabil make it suitable for use on fields other than grass. Photographs and drawings of Patrick cleats are used by permission of Action & Leisure, Inc.

they buy in regular shoes. When buying shoes, make sure the child wears the socks he or she will wear in the shoes. If the child wears two pairs of socks when playing, buy the shoes to fit with two pairs of socks. Poor quality shoes often come only in full sizes, and sometimes the right and left shoes are of different sizes!

Encourage your child to break new shoes in gradually. The shoes need time to adjust themselves to the feet. The child who wears new shoes for the first time in a game risks blisters and bruised toes and usually will not be able to play a full 90 minutes.

Andrew Clues explains how some professionals break in new shoes. They put on two pairs of socks and lace the new shoes up comfortably over them. They then immerse their feet in buckets of warm water for a half hour or so, during which time the water molds the leather of the shoes to the contours of the feet. Then the shoes are taken off and allowed to air dry naturally (*not* baked in an oven). Vogelsinger points out that this water treatment speeds the process of breaking in shoes.

Players in competitive soccer may need two pairs of shoes — one for dry fields and one (with longer studs) for wet. Artificial turf and indoor play also require special shoes. Figure 3.2 shows a couple of shoe styles. Figure 3.4 shows a shoe suited for indoor soccer. If your child plays on a variety of surfaces, and you can afford only one pair of shoes, buy shoes with a molded sole and smaller studs. The smaller studs may give a bit less traction, but they can add to the child's safety by preventing twisted knees from turning quickly or from being tackled hard by an opponent.

As a rule, expect to replace shoes every year. If the child doesn't outgrow them, mud, water, and hard use will probably damage them. When your child begins the rapid growth that comes with puberty, you may have to replace the shoes twice a year.

Paul Harris recommends not buying very high-priced shoes unless your child is the first soccer player in a family of twelve future players! However, the child who plays a great deal of competitive soccer may need the greater comfort, protection, and durability that some higher-priced shoes offer. Some soccer associations maintain a used shoe exchange to help players acquire good shoes inexpensively.

To extend the life of the shoes, clean them after use with saddle soap, especially if the shoes have gotten wet and muddy, and use leather polish on them. Sports stores sell oil-based mixtures that players can rub into the leather to increase its suppleness. Dust the insides of the shoes regularly with talcum powder to lessen the chance of infection. Use an innersole to prevent jarring on hard ground. And to prevent a lace from breaking in the middle of a game, change the laces regularly.

# Shinguards

Although today's shinguards (shin pads) are lightweight and flexible, many players resist them because it takes a bit of time to get used to them. Vogelsinger has just two words to say on the subject: "Wear them!" Shinguards are made of canvas, simulated leather, or plastic. The plastic ones (Figure 3.3) are usually molded, with a soft foam or sponge backing, and are available in several calf sizes. Some come with a strap and Velcro fastener to keep the guard on the leg. Others depend on a close-fitting sock to keep the shinguard in place.

In plastic shinguards, which are approximately 5½ to 6 inches wide, children aged 7-12 usually need the school children's size, which is about 6 inches high. Youths 12 to 15 years usually need the youth size, which is about 7 inches high. From 15 on up, players usually need an adult size, which is about 8 inches high.

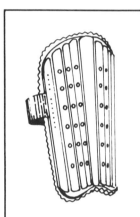

**Fig. 3.3-A** Plastic shinguard fastens around player's leg, under sock. Picture used by permission of Union Jacks.

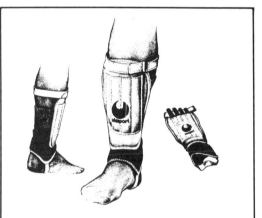

**Fig. 3.3-B** Tibia Tri-Safe shinguard protects the shin, ankle, and Achilles tendon. An elastic stirrup holds the shinguard down on the ankle. A Velcro and elastic band holds the guard snugly around the shin. Picture of shinguard used with permission of Uhlsport, Action & Leisure, Inc.

Players who resist using shinguards are often quite happy with a fitted "Soc-guard" of heavy-duty Antron/Lycra spandex fabric with padding inside (made by the Trace Athletic Corporation of Bellevue, Washington). This shinguard, which comes in several colors and sizes, slips on like a sock, with a wide elastic band under the foot, and can be worn with other socks either under or over it. Its socklike structure keeps it in place, and it washes just like socks do.

Still another type, the Tibia Tri-Safe (Figure 3.3B), protects the shin, ankle, and Achilles tendon. A bit more costly than other shinguards, it is still an excellent investment, especially for competitive soccer players.

Whatever kind you choose, insist that your child wear shinguards for all practices and games. A kick in the shins can be very painful and may discourage a child from continuing with soccer. If he or she complains that many professional players don't wear them, point out that those players have had many years of learning how to avoid injuries.

# Socks

Socks should reach to just below the player's knee to protect the player from scrapes and bruises and to keep the muscles warm. Socks come in two types: self-holding stretch and those with turnover tops held up by elastic ties or garters. The stretch socks are best for children and youths; they keep plastic shinguards snugly in place, and players (or parents) don't have to keep track of the garters.

Many experts recommend wearing two pairs of socks to cushion the foot a bit more and allow the skin to breathe better. The inside pair should be light; the outside pair, heavier and more absorbent. A bit of talcum powder on the skin under the socks also increases foot comfort.

**Fig. 3.4** This fully uniformed player is wearing socks with turn-down tops. Note this player's choice of a shoe without studs for indoor soccer. Picture used by permission of Union Jacks.

# Jerseys, Shorts, and Sweat Outfits

Parents usually have little say about uniforms, especially when the child plays in a well-established program. However, if you have the chance to influence the choice of shirts and shorts, look for:

- Strong, careful stitching and sturdy collars and cuffs.
- Bright, long-lasting colors.
- Lightweight fabrics that 1) resist stain, 2) can be machine washed and dried, and 3) "breathe" to release sweat and heat, keeping players cool. Many coaches and players prefer a 50/50 cotton/polyester blend for shirts.
- Shorts with good elastic waistbands, split side seams, ample room for movement (avoid skintight pants), and (for boys) a built-in underpant/supporter. Even if you can't get your son to wear a youth athletic supporter, the underpant will provide some protection by holding his testicles close to the body.
- Attractive styling that appeals to the players.
- Reversibility of jerseys, so your child gets two uniforms for the price of one.

In Fig. 3.5-A, note that one shirt is dark and the other light. Most competitive teams have one dark and one light shirt (say white on blue and blue on white) because they often play other teams whose uniforms are the same color as theirs. Without contrasting shirts, neither the players nor the officials can quickly tell one team from the other. Part C shows not only the dark/light contrast but also short-and long-sleeved uniforms. Figure 3.4 shows still another, as do other pictures in the book.

Sweat pants and tops aren't essential, although they are useful for practices, and in cooler weather they keep players warm while they are on the sidelines. Like uniforms, sweat outfits should be sturdy with strong stitching, brightly colored, and machine washable and dryable. When choosing style, consider the ease with which players will be able to slip the suit off and on before entering and after leaving a game.

Also consider visibility — some children will wear their sweat suits as they walk or bicycle to and from practice. A suit with large amounts of white or a light color is more visible than a dark suit, especially at and after sundown. Light colors are particularly important for dark-skinned players, who are almost invisible in the dark when they wear dark sweat suits.

**Fig. 3.5-A** Two different styles of shirt — with collar and without, dark and light.

**Fig. 3.5-B** A typical pair of soccer shorts. Pictures used by permission of Umbro Soccer Education Division.

**Fig. 3.5-C** Uniformed players show still more of the variety in uniform styles as does the uniform in Figure 3.4. Picture used by permission of Union Jacks.

**Fig. 3.6** This goalie, poised to receive a shot, is wearing a goalkeeper's suit with special padding on the knees and elbows (to provide protection during dives). Also note the gloves, which help goalkeepers to grasp the ball securely. The photograph is used by permission of Uhlsport, Action & Leisure, Inc.

## Goalkeeper's Equipment

Because goalkeepers have special duties and privileges, they wear jerseys that distinguish them from both their own and all opposing players. Their jerseys usually have padding over the elbows to protect them during dives (Figure 3.6). Goalkeepers' pants also have protective padding over the hips and knees. If necessary, elbow and knee pads can be bought separately. Because rain or cold weather can make the ball hard to handle, many goalkeepers use special gloves.

## Other Equipment

Many coaches recommend that boys wear an athletic supporter. Some want boys to wear a supporter with a protective cup. Similarly, dentists recommend a personally fitted mouthpiece, especially for goalkeepers. And if your child wears braces, ask the dentist for protective wax strips, to press onto the metal before practices and games, to prevent cuts inside the lips.

Various kinds of body protectors are available for elbows, groin, knees, and so forth. Most are foam-padded and lightweight. One caution: if your child uses protectors, make certain that he or she isn't just covering up an injury that needs treatment.

In addition, ball-inflating equipment, such as needles, flat-proof sealant, and a bicycle pump, is always useful. Another item that is useful, but not essential, is a backyard practice goal made of steel pipe with stakes and durable nylon nets.

A "tether" or "pendulum" ball, that attaches to a rope by means of a swivel, is good for practicing heading and kicking. With this device the height of the ball can be adjusted depending on which skill the player wants to practice (Figure 3.7). A similar unit is a soccer ball on a tether that is attached to a player's foot and allows him or her to practice kicking without having to run great distances to retrieve the ball.

## Forbidden Equipment

Players are forbidden to wear any equipment that might harm an opponent. This includes watches, jewelry, hard casts, and the like.

**Fig. 3.7** Players practice kicking and heading with pendulum balls. Note that balls are at different heights, depending on the skill the player wants to practice. Picture used by permission of Hubert Vogelsinger, Puma All-Star Soccer School.

# Soccer Skills

To make specific skills easy to find, this chapter lists trapping (controlling) and foot skills first, other ball movement skills next, body skills and throw-ins next, and goaltending skills last. This is not necessarily the order in which your child is likely to learn the skills.

As Vogelsinger points out, skills are most likely to be taught in the following groups and order:

- Kicking, passing, and shooting.
- Trapping and ball control.
- Heading.
- Dribbling and feinting.

## Trapping and Ball Control

Trapping, done with any part of the body except the hands, is the soccer player's way of bringing the ball under control. Trapping cushions the impact of the ball and guides it to the ground for kicking or dribbling. In general, the higher the ball is off the ground, the harder it is to control. Figure 4.1 shows a trap with the bottom of the foot.

The chest trap (crossed arms over the chest are allowed in some girls' competition), shown in Figure 4.2, drops the ball directly at the player's feet. In the leg trap, (Figure 1.2, Chapter 1), the player uses any part of the leg to knock the ball down. Players also use thigh traps (Figure 4.3), knee traps, inside-of-foot traps, and shin traps.

**Fig. 4.1** Hubert Vogelsinger, well-known soccer player and coach, shows a young player the proper technique for a sole-of-foot trap. Above photo and photos on next three pages by S. Frinzi; used by permission of Hubert Vogelsinger, Puma All-Star Soccer School.

**Fig. 4.2** Vogelsinger shows a player the proper technique for controlling the ball on the chest.

**Fig. 4.3** Indiana University player controls the ball on her thigh. Picture used by permission of Indiana University Women's Soccer Club.

# Kicking

Kicking is one of several ways to move the ball from one place to another. Accurate kicking requires attention to the ball's surface and the foot's position. A player can kick the ball in any of four places as it faces him or her: in the center, below center, or left or right of center. Kicking the ball in dead center propels the ball low and forward. Kicking below center moves the ball forward in a rising arc. A kick to the left of center will send the ball to the right; a kick on the right will move it left.

Although it often seems strange at first to children and parents alike, soccer players kick with the toe only when the only way to reach a ball *is* with the toe. The reason is that kicking with the toe puts only about a square inch of the foot on the ball, giving the player very little control over where the ball goes.

The proper surfaces with which to kick the ball are, in rough order of frequency of use, the inside of the foot (which is used 75% of the time and provides the largest striking area), the full instep (where the shoe is laced up), and the outside of the instep. Occasionally players kick the ball with the heel. The pictures in Figure 4.4 illustrate the inside-of-foot kick.

The instep kick, the most powerful kick in soccer, is often used for goal shots. Figure 4.5 shows where the ball should meet the foot and how to move the foot to the ball and kick it.

The outside-of-foot kick enables the player to kick the ball with a curve in it (indeed, the curve has caused it to be nicknamed the "banana kick"). Figure 4.6 shows where the ball should meet the foot.

If you wish to work on kicks with your child, get one of the coaching books recommended in the bibliography to use as a guide. Also, have your child's coach demonstrate proper technique with your child.

To help your child get a feel for the ball, encourage barefooted practice in the back yard. Bare feet discourage kicking with the toe — it hurts!

**Fig. 4.4-A** Hubert Vogelsinger shows a player the correct position for an inside-of-foot kick. Above photo and those on following seven pages by S. Frinzi; used by permission of Hubert Vogelsinger, Puma All-Star Soccer School.

**Fig. 4.4-B** Under the watchful eye of a coach, this player practices an inside-of-foot kick on a pendulum ball.

**Fig. 4.5-A** Vogelsinger shows where the ball meets the foot on an instep kick.

**Fig. 4.5-B** Vogelsinger shows how to move the foot toward the ball on an instep kick.

**Fig. 4.5-C** Player executes instep kick.

**Fig. 4.6** Vogelsinger helps player position himself for outside-of-foot kick.

# Dribbling

Dribbling, or running with the ball, moves the ball by a series of gentle taps while keeping it under control. Good dribbling requires players to have a "feel" for the ball. Players often use both the inside of the toe and the outside as dribbling surfaces. Less often (because it's harder to control) they use the top and the bottom of the toe. How hard and where they touch the ball depends on where they want the ball to go.

Figure 4.7 shows players dribbling the ball through a series of cones. Usually, as the pictures also show, dribblers keep the ball directly at their feet because if the ball is out in front of them, they risk having an opponent steal it.

**Fig. 4.7-A** Player practices dribbling through a series of cones. To get players to look up while dribbling, substitute bicycle flags for the cones. Picture used by permission of Puma All-Star Soccer School.

**Fig. 4.7·B** Indiana University soccer player dribbles toward goal. Picture used by permission of Indiana University men's soccer coach.

# Volleying and Half-Volleying

Volleying and half-volleying also move the ball from one place to another on the field. A player volleys by passing or shooting a ball without first trapping and controlling it. Thus, volleys are hard to perform accurately. A half-volley occurs when a player kicks the ball after a short bounce. Figure 4.8 shows players practicing the volley.

**Fig. 4.8** Player practices a volley kick by placing the ball on top of a cone. Picture used by permission of Hubert Vogelsinger, Puma All-Star Soccer School.

# Shooting

Players score goals by kicking or heading the ball over the goal line into the net. The most powerfully kicked shot is made with the full instep. The toe points toward the ground, and the ankle is locked. As the kicking foot hits the ball, the toe lightly brushes the ground. Good follow-through provides extra power. The balance foot stands closer to the ball than in other kicks and points toward the goal.

# Heading

Heading, like kicking, dribbling, and volleying, is just a way of moving the ball. To many children and parents, heading the ball seems an unnatural act. However, heading can be painless and accurate when a player hits the ball with his or her forehead and makes contact at the highest point of the jump. The secret to getting power and distance is for players to strike the ball rather than letting it strike them. Players control direction by turning the head in the direction the ball is to go.

**Fig. 4.9-A** Indiana University soccer player grimaces as he heads the ball. Picture used by permission of Indiana University men's soccer team.

**Fig. 4.9-B** Coach Vogelsinger shows a young player where the ball should touch him when he is heading the ball—on the forehead, between the eyes. Photo by S. Frinzi; used by permission of Puma All-Star Soccer School.

**Fig. 4.9-C** Player stretches out for a flying header. Picture used by permission of Puma All-Star Soccer School.

# Juggling

Juggling helps players to become comfortable with the ball, learning how to handle and control it without hands. As the pictures in Figure 4.10 show, juggling keeps the ball in the air by bouncing it off the top of a player's toes, thigh, shoulders, head — anyplace except hands and arms. My son's coach sometimes holds a juggling contest during practice. The player that keeps the ball in the air the longest wins a pizza.

**Fig. 4.10** These pictures show the technique of juggling the ball, which many players consider more fun than practice. The photo above and the one opposite are used by permission of Umbro Soccer Education Division.

The photo at left and below and those on the following four pages feature the technique of juggling as taught at the Puma All Star Soccer School. Photos by S. Frinzi and used by permission of the School.

# Passing

Passing systematically transfers the ball from one player to another. Commonly done with the feet, players can also pass by heading the ball to a teammate. Typically, the player directs the ball toward an open space into which a teammate arrives at the same moment as the ball.

Your child will probably learn the "push pass" first. This pass, made by using the inside of the foot, is the most reliable passing method because the ball makes contact with the broadest part of the foot. The player shown in Figure 7.2 (Chapter 7) is probably practicing the push pass.

One special type of pass, the "wall" pass (Figure 4.11, Part A), resembles the "give-and-go" in basketball. Player A passes the ball to teammate B, who volleys back to A at a point farther down the field. By using the volley (one action) rather than trapping and then passing (two actions), B is acting much like a wall (hence the name). The wall pass is very useful for getting the ball around defenders, such as the X in Figure 4.11, who are directly in the path of the ball carrier.

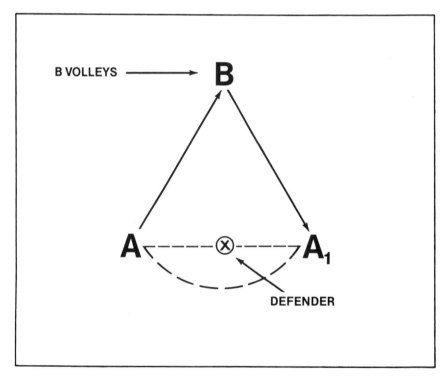

**Fig. 4.11-A** In this diagram, B is acting like a "wall" for A, who kicks the ball and runs forward to receive the volley back from B.

**Fig. 4.11-B** Indiana University player 18 directs a short pass to a teammate. Picture used by permission of Indiana University Women's Soccer Club.

**Fig. 4.11-C** Indiana player (hair in scarf) "crosses" a pass in front of the goal to a teammate (not shown) who has a better shot at the goal. Picture used by permission of Indiana University Women's Soccer Club.

# Charging and Shielding

Charging, used to set up a steal, is legal only when the ball is within playing distance and contact is made shoulder to shoulder. The player who charges hopes to come away with the ball. A player who charges must be going for the ball, not the opponent. A charge aimed more at the opponent usually draws a whistle and a foul call.

Shielding the ball — placing one's body between the ball and the opponent — is an excellent way to protect the ball while deciding what to do with it. An often-neglected basic skill, shielding may prevent an opponent from playing a ball that is headed out of bounds. It may also allow another defender to intercept the ball and make an unhindered play.

# Marking and Tackling

Often you'll hear the coach call out, "Mark your man!" or "Mark up! Mark up!" Marking is man-to-man guarding, much like that in basketball. The defender's purpose is to intercept a pass, to tackle and knock the ball away from an opponent, or to play so closely that passes won't even be sent to the marked player.

Unlike football tackling, soccer tackling is aimed at the ball. The would-be tackler may reach for the ball with one foot, jump for it with

**Fig. 4.12-A** Player executes sliding tackle during game. Picture used by permission of adidas USA Inc.

both feet, or slide toward the ball with one or both feet, much as a baseball player slides for the plate. The purpose is to push the ball away from the opponent into control of another defender. The pictures in Figure 4.12 show both a sliding tackle (Part A) and a standing tackle (Part B).

Players who try a sliding tackle need to be pretty sure of success; failure means that the tackler is temporarily out of the play while he or she stands up. Getting up is easier when the tackler uses a "bent-leg" technique. The player bends the bottom leg going into the tackle. Coming out, he or she digs the cleats into the ground and uses the momentum to push the body back to a standing position.

An improper tackle, one that is aimed at an opponent, not the ball, will usually draw a whistle from the referee. Tackles aimed at the opponent can cause unhappiness and injury. Referees try to protect players by being very strict about penalizing teams for improper tackling.

**Fig. 4.12-B** Indiana University soccer player (white uniform) tackles an opponent to gain control of the ball. Picture used by permission of Indiana University's men's soccer team.

# Throwing In

The throw-in is used to put the ball back into play after it has gone out of bounds over a side line. It is a two-handed pass to a teammate, done with both hands from behind the head. Both feet must be on the ground out of bounds or on the sidelines. Some players take a running start to add power to the throw, but at the moment the throw is made, both feet must be touching the ground.

# Feinting (Faking)

Feinting, or faking, occurs when a player pretends to move one way and then goes another. The purpose is to mislead defensive players into committing themselves to move in the direction the faking player does *not* plan to go. Players feint with the head, the body, and the feet. One common fake involves a move to pass in one direction followed by dribbling off in another.

My son's coach cautions players to keep their eyes on their opponent's bellybutton. "Whichever way that goes, the rest of him will follow." A fake must be followed by a move around the opponent or it becomes meaningless.

# Running "Off the Ball" and Seeing the Field

At any given time, only one player will have the ball. The job of teammates who don't have the ball is to run skillfully "off the ball," and get free of players who are marking them; they, thus, become able to receive a pass.

Closely related is the skill of seeing the field. At all times players need to know not only their own position but also where their teammates are and where spaces on the field are opening up. A player who has good field vision and who moves well off the ball makes things happen on the field.

Both skills depend to a great extent on the skill, vision, and unselfishness of teammates. A player who creates openings but never receives a pass will soon be discouraged.

# Goaltending

The goalkeeper is the last man on defense and often the first on offense. The keeper's position relative to the penalty area is crucial to defense. Although new soccer fans often worry about how far from the goal the goalkeeper often plays, under many circumstances playing out cuts down the likelihood of a successful shot on goal.

To stop a shot, goalkeepers will often jump for a high ball or dive for a low one (Figure 4.13, Part A and Part B). They can kick, punch, or deflect the ball away from the goal mouth. Also, goalies, unlike other players, can catch the ball with their hands.

Although dives often put the goalie's face right in the midst of a nest of kicking feet (hence the reputation that good goalies are a bit crazy), Vogelsinger comments that injuries rarely occur when a goalkeeper moves swiftly and decisively. Hesitation is much more likely to result in injury. Sometimes the goalie catches the ball. When that's not possible, the preferred move is to punch it hard away from the goal. When the goalie catches the ball, he or she gets rid of it with a hard kick or throw up the field toward the opposite goal.

**Fig. 4.13-A** Goalkeeper dives to his right for a save. Photo by S. Frinzi; used by permission of Puma All-Star Soccer School.

**Fig. 4.13-B** Keeper dives to his left for a save. Photo used by permission of Puma All-Star Soccer School.

**Fig. 5.1-A** This properly uniformed referee wears the traditional black and white shirt, pants, and socks. The game ball is in his left hand and a whistle in the right. Beside him is a small wallet that holds game report forms. On his left wrist is a watch with a timer. Photo used by permission of Union Jacks.

# The Laws
# Of Soccer

Soccer's 17 laws are simple enough to learn. The problem is, they aren't simple to apply, as I learned when our son Rob took the courses and tests needed to qualify as a soccer official. When he returned from class each evening, he regaled us with stories about hypothetical game situations. Here is a brief summary of FIFA (pronounced "FeeFah") rules.

## Law No. 1 — Soccer Field

The beginning of Chapter 2 (Figure 2.1) shows a regulation soccer field with minimum and maximum dimensions and parts marked.

## Law No. 2 — Ball

The ball must be round and properly inflated. Figure 3.1 shows soccer balls in different sizes. For international play, the ball must have a circumference of 27 to 28 inches and must weigh 14 to 16 ounces.

## Law No. 3 — Number of Players

A team is composed of eleven players, one of whom is the goalkeeper. Before the start of a game, the coach should list all players, including substitutes, and their numbers on a roster card and give it to the referee.

# Law No. 4—Players' Equipment

No player may carry or wear onto the field anything (such as a watch, chain, bracelet, hard cast, metal studs on cleats, etc.) that might injure another player. Goalkeepers must wear clothes that clearly distinguish them from all other players.

# Laws No. 5 and 6—Officials

One referee officiates at each game. He has absolute authority to enforce rules, decide disputes, eject players, and even to stop a game if the coach or the crowd becomes too unruly. (Referees cannot declare a forfeit in this case; they can only stop the game or declare it unplayable. Authorities of the league sponsoring the game must then decide the result.)

Two linesmen (side referees) equipped with small flags assist the game referee by 1) indicating when the ball has left the field of play and 2) signaling which team is to be awarded corner kicks, side throw-ins, and goal kicks. In addition, the linesmen signal off-side violations (see Law No. 11) and fouls that the referee might not have seen. However, the referee has the final decision and may overrule a linesman on any call.

Officials wear a simple black uniform with white trim. Figure 5.1-A shows a properly uniformed referee. Below is some of the referee's equipment. The carry bag stores an official's gear neatly and is ready to go at a moment's notice.

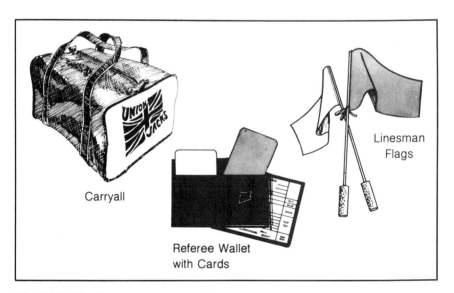

Carryall

Referee Wallet
with Cards

Linesman
Flags

**Fig. 5.1-B** The linesmen use these flags to signal their calls. The wallet holds game reports. The bag holds all a referee's gear, ready to go at a moment's notice. Drawings used by permission of Union Jacks.

## Law No. 7 — Duration of Game

FIFA rules specify two equal periods of 45 minutes each and a half-time period of 5 minutes. Young children's games are shorter. For instance, teams of children 5 to 8 years old often play four 10-minute quarters or two 20-minute halves. Rob's Under-14 league often played 40-minute halves. Tournament games are sometimes shorter than regulation because teams are playing two or three games a day.

On very hot days, referees may decide to play quarters rather than halves to lessen the risk of illness due to heat.

## Law No. 8 — Start of Play

Referees use a coin toss to decide which team has the choice of either kicking off or picking the goal it wishes to defend. The game starts when the referee signals and a player kicks the ball from the center spot into the opponent's part of the field. On a kick off, the ball must be played *forward* from its original spot by at least its full circumference before another player may touch it. The player who kicks off cannot touch the ball again until it has been touched by another player.

After a goal is scored, play is restarted in the same way by the team that didn't score. After half-time, play is started in the same way by the team that didn't kick off at the beginning of the game.

If play is stopped at any time for reasons such as injury to a player, the referee restarts play by dropping the ball between two opposing players.

## Law No. 9 — Ball In and Out of Play

The ball is in play until it completely crosses an out-of-bounds line or goal line. If *any* part of the ball is touching the line, it is still in play. If the ball touches the referee while on the field of play or rebounds from a goal post into the field of play, action continues.

## Law No. 10 — Method of Scoring

A goal is scored when the entire ball crosses over the goal line between the goal posts and under the crossbar provided the ball was not propelled by an offensive player's hand or arm or was not the result of an indirect free kick, a goal kick, a kick off, or a throw-in. The team scoring the greatest number of goals wins.

# Law No. 11—Off-Side

The off-side rule has probably confused more people than any other rule except, perhaps, the "advantage rule" (see below). A player is off-side when he or she is nearer to the opponent's goal than the ball is *at or prior to the moment the ball is passed* unless:

- The player is in his or her own half of the field of play.
- Two opponents (usually the goalie and one field player) are nearer to their own goal than the player is.
- The ball was last touched or played by a member of the defensive team.
- The player receives the ball directly from a goal kick, corner kick, throw in, or drop ball by the referee.
- The player has clearly removed himself from the play and is, therefore, not giving him- or herself an "advantage" over the opponent by being off-side.

Violation of the off-side rule is devilishly hard for novices to spot because 1) the player must be judged to be trying to gain an unfair advantage and 2) the violation occurs at the moment the ball is *played*, not *received*. The penalty for being off-side is an indirect free kick for the defenders.

On defense, some teams will deliberately try to trap the offensive team in an off-side position by moving their players up the field just far enough to ensure that there are not two defenders between the farthest forward offensive player and the goal. This maneuver is called the "off-side trap."

**A: OFF-SIDE**

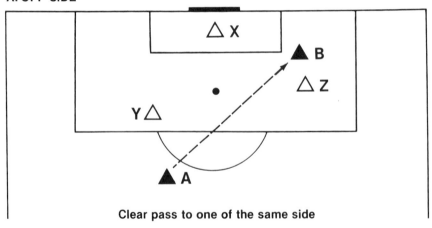

**Clear pass to one of the same side**

*A is in possession of the ball, and having Y in front, passes to B.*
*B is off-side because he is in front of A and there are not two opponents between him and the goal-line when the ball is passed by A.*
*If B waits for Z to fall back before he shoots, this will not put him on-side, because it does not alter his position with relation to A at the moment the ball was passed by A.*

**Fig. 5.2-A** and **5.2-B** are illustrations of off-side position. Fig. 5.2-A shows a pass from player A to player B. B is off-side because at the time of the pass, only the goalie is between B and the goal line.

## B: OFF-SIDE

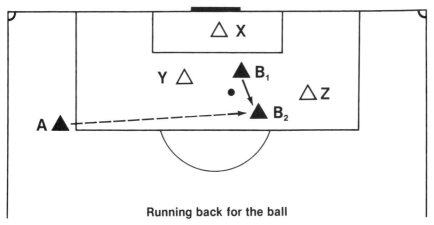

**Running back for the ball**

*A centers the ball. B runs back from position 1 to position 2, and then dribbles between Y and Z and scores.*
*B is off-side because he is in front of the ball and did not have two opponents between him and the goal-line at the moment the ball was played by A.*

**Fig. 5.2-B** A centers the ball and B runs back to receive it. Again, B is off-side because at the time of the play, only the goalie is between B and the goal. It makes no difference that B has two opponents between him and the goal when he touches the ball. Off-side position is determined when the ball is *played*, not when it is received.

## NOT OFF-SIDE

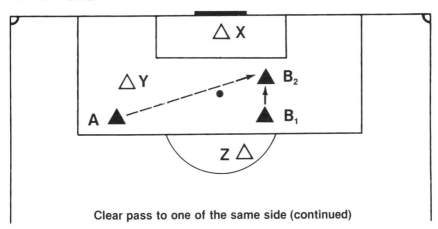

**Clear pass to one of the same side (continued)**

*A is in possession of the ball, and having Y in front, passes across the field. B runs from position 1 to position 2.*
*B is not off-side because at the moment the ball was passed by A, he was not in front of the ball, and had two opponents between him and the goal-line.*

**Fig. 5.3** This diagram illustrates on-side position. At the time A plays the ball, B has two players between herself and the goal line. As soon as the ball is played. B runs forward for a shot on goal. B is not off-side because at the time the ball was played, two players stood between him and the goal line.

# aw No. 12—Fouls and Misconduct

### dvantage Rule"

The "Advantage Rule" is a basic principle that helps referees to decide when to penalize a team. Unlike basketball and American football, the referee isn't trying to penalize a team for *all* fouls and acts of misconduct. Instead, the purpose is to keep the game going by penalizing only acts that work to the *disadvantage* of the team against whom the act was committed.

Suppose your daughter has the ball and is moving in for a shot on goal. The defending fullback tries to stop the shot by kicking her in the leg. Somehow she continues on, regaining her balance, shooting, and scoring. Even though kicking is a major foul, the referee probably won't call it. After all, your daughter scored, and it would be a *disadvantage* to her team if the referee called the foul and took away the goal.

Take another situation. Your son is dribbling down field, and a defender charges him from behind. Your son stumbles but retains control of the ball and keeps dribbling or passes successfully to a teammate. Again, the defender committed a foul, but an experienced referee won't call it because it is to the *advantage* of your son's team not to have the foul called. If the defender had managed to extract the ball from your son, the foul would have been called at the moment the defender gained possession.

Sometimes referees raise a hand at the time a foul is committed to signal their awareness of the foul to players, coaches, and observers. The call will await the outcome of play. If the team that was fouled manages to retain control, the referee will often call out "Play on" to signal that no foul will be called.

This philosophy differs radically from that of basketball, where a defender will sometimes foul to keep the offense from scoring. In basketball, as long as the foul occurs before the shot (and the referee calls it a foul), the goal will not be allowed, even if the shot goes in.

In short, the next time your child is fouled and the referee doesn't call it, take a second look. Calling the foul might have hurt your child's team.

### The Acts

There are nine forbidden acts for which the referee can award a *direct free-kick* to the offended team. "Direct" means that the ball may be played directly into the opponent's goal. The first three offenses are committed with the feet; the next two, with the body; and the last four, with the hands. All except the hand ball are committed against an opponent.

- Kicking or trying to kick an opponent.
- Tripping.
- Jumping.
- Charging violently or dangerously.
- Charging from behind (unless the opponent is obstructing).
- Holding.
- Pushing.
- Striking or trying to strike.
- Handling the ball (for field players, any time; for the goalkeeper, when outside the penalty area).

All fouls must be judged to have been intentional. For this reason you may sometimes hear the referee say "Play on" to signal awareness of the foul combined with the judgment that it was not committed with intention.

A direct free-kick is taken from the spot where the foul occurred unless an offensive player commits a foul in the defending team's goal area. In that case, the defensive player takes a free-kick from any point within that half of the goal area in which the foul occurred.

When a defensive player, however, commits an intentional foul inside his or her own penalty area, the referee may award a penalty-kick to the offense.

The awarding of a penalty kick, and sometimes a direct kick, usually causes several players on the defending team to link arms and huddle close together to build a wall in front of the goal between the goal and the spot where the ball is to be kicked. To protect themselves, boys usually cup their hands over their testicles. With younger children especially, this formation can make the participants look as if all of them suddenly and urgently need a trip to the bathroom.

When a player commits an infraction of the laws (as opposed to a foul), the penalty is an *indirect free-kick*, which means that no goal can be scored directly by that kick. Rather, another player must first touch the ball. Infractions include:

- Playing in a manner considered dangerous, such as kicking high or trying to kick the ball *while* the goalkeeper is holding it.
- Charging a player who is not within playing distance of the ball and who is not trying to play the ball.
- When not playing the ball, intentionally obstructing an opponent.
- Charging the goalkeeper (except when the keeper is holding the ball, is obstructing an opponent, or has passed outside the goal area).

- Goalkeepers only: 1) taking more than four steps while holding, bouncing, or throwing the ball in the air and catching it again without releasing it totally, or, 2) in the opinion of the referee, wasting time and delaying the game so as to give his or her team an unfair advantage.

An indirect free-kick may also be awarded, and the offending player cautioned, when a player:

- Enters, reenters, or leaves the field of play during the game without having received the appropriate signal from the referee.
- Persistently breaks the Laws of the Game.
- Shows, by word or action, disagreement with any decision of the referee.
- Is guilty of inappropriate conduct.

Referees can discipline players in one of three ways: 1) verbal warning, 2) showing a yellow card, and 3) showing a red card. A verbal warning simply tells a player to watch his behavior. Receiving a yellow card is more serious. Players never receive the yellow card twice because on the second such offense, the referee shows the red card and puts the player out of the game. Showing the red card, even if it has not been preceded by a verbal warning and/or a yellow card, automatically puts the offending player out of the game, and his or her team plays short-handed for the remainder of the game.

Players may be banished from the game with no prior warning for:

- In the referee's opinion, committing a serious foul or conducting themselves violently.
- Using foul or abusive language.
- Persisting in misconduct.

# Law No. 13—Free-Kick (Direct and Indirect)

On a *direct free-kick*, a goal may be scored without the ball's having touched another player. A goal cannot be scored directly from an *indirect free-kick*. When a player takes a free-kick anywhere on the field, all opponents must stay outside a ten-yard radius from the ball until the ball is in play unless they are standing on their own goal line between the goal posts.

# Law No. 14—Penalty Kick

A penalty kick is awarded to the opponents when the defending team commits one of the nine direct fouls (described earlier) within its own penalty area. All players except the kicker and the goalie must be outside the penalty area and at least ten yards from the penalty mark. The goalie must stand on his or her own goal line between the goal posts and is not allowed to move the feet before the ball is kicked.

## Law No. 15 — Throw-In

When a ball goes out of bounds over a sideline, it is thrown back into play by an opponent of the team that last touched the ball. Both of the thrower's feet must be touching the ground either on or outside the sideline. He or she must face the field and throw in a motion that uses both hands and brings the ball from behind and over the head.

## Law No. 16 — Goal Kick

When an offensive player kicks the ball past the goal line but not into the goal, the defending team is awarded a "goal kick," which is taken from any place within the goal area (the smaller area shown on Figure 2.1). The ball is placed in the goal area nearest the side on which the ball went out of bounds, and usually, it is the fullback or halfback who takes the goal kick. Opposing players must stay outside the penalty area until the ball has left the penalty area.

## Law No. 17 — Corner Kick

When a defensive player is the last one to touch a ball that goes over the goal line but not into the goal, the offensive team is awarded a corner kick. The kicker plays the ball in from the "corner circle" or "quarter arc" nearest the place where the ball went out of bounds. A goal may be scored directly from a corner kick.

# Tactics and Strategy

Good soccer is beautifully, gracefully, and intelligently played. You'll appreciate it more if you know a few of the principles that govern tactics and strategy.

Soccer offense depends on the creation and exploitation of space, especially the area in front of the goal mouth, which Vogelsinger calls "decisive space." The offense aims to put an open man with the ball in the decisive space. The defense tries to prevent that occurrence. If you want to know more about offensive and defensive tactics, read Chapters 5 and 10 in Vogelsinger's *The Challenge of Soccer* or any of the coaching books recommended in the bibliography. Some of the ideas discussed below come from Vogelsinger's chapters.

## Offense

### Simplicity, Space, and Improvisation

Simplicity and space are crucial to the offense. Unlike American football, soccer play doesn't stop when the ball changes sides, and fouls don't usually stop the clock. Since there are no time-outs, plays can't be sent in from the sidelines, and coaching from the sidelines isn't very effective. Improvisation and creativity, then, are keys to soccer plays. Intelligence, creativity, basic skills, and fitness are far more important factors than knowledge of various plays.

Unless the offense has managed a breakaway, players will be crowded around the goal when someone is trying to score. To score, the offense has to clear a space to get the ball through. Watch for these spaces. When the offensive play is working as it should, you'll see the ball passed to the space just in time to meet an offensive player who is moving into it. A score may follow, often as the result of a quick, low shot or a header into the corner of the goal.

### Triangle Patterns and Depth

When players are moving the ball down field, watch for triangle patterns in the players' positions. Sometimes players' formation sets up a series of linking triangles all the way down a field, as in Figure 9.1. These triangles produce depth by giving the offense a path along which to move the ball toward the opponent's goal. The popular wall pass pattern (or give-and-go), illustrated in Chapter 4, forms a triangle. In Figure 6.1, G is the goalie, B stands for fullbacks, H for halfbacks, and F for forwards. From the person nearest the goal, every player can act as the point of at least two triangles, and the back halfback and the back forward (the halfback and forward closest to their own goal) are points in four triangles each. As long as the players stay in roughly this same relationship to each other, even though the formation as a whole is moving up and down the field, all players know who is likely to pass to them and who is a good candidate to receive a pass.

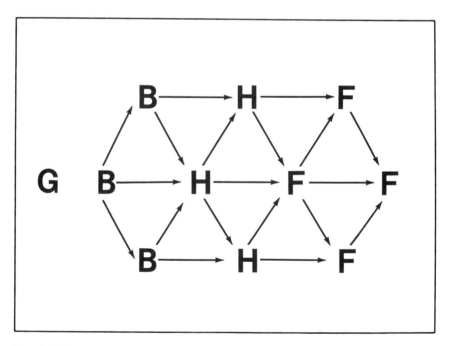

**Fig. 6.1** Note the triangles formed by drawing lines that connect players.

You'll notice both long passes, sometimes effective in setting up a breakaway (rather like the outlet pass that starts a fast break in basketball), and short passes, which enable the offense to move the ball despite close guarding. The most accurate way to pass or score is on the ground. Indeed, you can tell a good team by how effectively the players execute ground passes. As players grow older, high balls aren't much of a threat.

Yet, certain playing conditions do enhance the value of high passes. For instance, when the weather has been very rainy, the field will be soggy. Even if the field is in good condition when a game starts, it will be rapidly churned up, especially in the middle, by the players' cleats. The wetter and more churned up the field, the harder it will be to pass accurately on the ground. A deep puddle will stop some passes completely. Under such conditions, high passes are often more effective, and players will try to move the ball down the sidelines to take advantage of the slightly better ground conditions there.

Humor can make such poor field conditions bearable. One Thanksgiving our team and an Under-14 team from our association played in a tournament in Tennessee. The fields were wet when the first games began on Friday, and by noon of the first day hard rain was falling again. The next afternoon, rain still coming down steadily, the Under-14 team was trying hard to move the ball out of the midfield. Footing was so poor that most players were covered with mud from frequent falls.

One of the midfielders, wary of falling again, practically tiptoed up to the ball, which was floating comfortably in a puddle. On nearing the ball he drew his right foot back and took a mighty swing, knowing that a gentle touch wouldn't get the ball out of the puddle. As he swung, though, the momentum caused him to lose his balance, and he wound up on his back in the puddle with the ball. At that, he and the other cold, wet players on both teams dissolved into uproarious laughter and a brief round of water fighting — something the players probably hadn't engaged in since early childhood. When the game ended a few minutes later, all players and spectators were still wet and cold, but grins and giggles were plentiful. For most participants, I suspect, tales of that game are going to be rather like stories of "the fish that got away": they'll improve with age and retelling.

## Support and Penetration

Good offense requires support for the forwards from the half-and fullbacks. The purpose of support is to get more offenders than defenders near the ball so that, no matter how tightly the defenders mark the offensive players, there will always be an offensive player who can get free and, possibly, score.

Penetration refers to progress up the field. Players often pass back and forth across the field, but in Vogelsinger's judgment, half of all passes should penetrate. When two possible passes exist, players should choose the one that will penetrate the greatest amount.

### Width and Mobility

In addition to support, strong offense also depends upon the right and left forwards (wing forwards) remaining in their outside positions. They give width to the attack and draw defenders out to cover them. Keeping distance between defensive players makes it harder for them to support each other, and that improves the offense's chances of scoring. Furthermore, when the wings move in, with their defenders marking them, they are likely to cause congestion in the goal area. This crowding makes scoring harder.

Constant mobility is crucial to creating and using space. When offensive players pass the ball and change positions constantly, they force defenders to decide whether to hold their positions or stay with the player they are marking. Making the wrong decision may open a space through which offense can move the ball for a score.

# Defense

Defense is central to soccer. If you doubt it, look at game scores. Scoring in double figures is rare, and in most games, neither team scores as many as five goals. Furthermore, the defense nearly always has an extra player because the offensive team's goalie is all the way at the other end of the field. (Sometimes, when a team desperately needs a goal, it will try to neutralize this disadvantage by pulling the goalkeeper out to act as an additional field player. Naturally, this increases the risk of a goal being scored by the other team.)

### Methods of Defense

Defensive players have the triple job of covering an opponent, covering for teammates, and covering space. Two common methods of defense — man-to-man marking (guarding) and zone play — may remind you of basketball. Man-to-man marking means that a defensive player tries to stay close enough to a specific offensive player to either prevent passes to that player or pick off any passes that are attempted. Zone defense, as the name implies, means that each player covers a roughly defined area rather than an offensive player. Vogelsinger prefers the zone defense for younger players because it is easier to learn and gives them more freedom.

The compound defense blends the zone and the man-to-man approaches. The compound defense has the advantage of flexibility, but it requires that players watch each other constantly and talk to each other as play progresses to make sure that each defender knows which players he or she is responsible for at any given moment.

### Principles of Defense

One important principle is **depth**, the purpose of which is to close gaps and to enable players to support each other. Defenders should avoid retreating in a straight line, because doing so leaves the space behind them vulnerable to a through pass.

**Delay**, also important, counters the offense's attempts at penetration and motion and gives time to fill gaps and position all defenders advantageously. **Concentration** around the penalty box counters the offensive team's attempts at width and helps to keep potential shooters at a decent distance from the goal.

**Balance** becomes important when an offensive player has beaten a defender. In such cases a teammate's shift to cover for the beaten defender may cause the defense as a whole to become unbalanced. The defenders must always be ready to reshuffle to correct imbalance.

Finally, the collective **control and restraint** required for good defense contrast sharply with the individuality and improvisation required for good offense. Defenders who let themselves be lured out of position or tricked into an early tackle risk disrupting the cohesiveness of the collective defensive effort.

One defensive tactic puzzled me the first time I saw it: a defender passing the ball back to his own goalie. Why would a defender kick toward his goal, possibly risking scoring *against* his team? As I watched, the answer became clear. First, it got the ball away from the offense. Second, it gave the goalie a chance to start an offensive drive. Third, it gave the goalie a chance to handle the ball, and to keep himself warmed up and ready for action. Getting warmed-up is especially important after a period of time when all the action has been taking place at the opposite end of the field.

# Rhythm or Blues

Rhythm is crucial to a game that depends on basic skills to produce close, coordinated passes. Your child's coach will undoubtedly use many drills and games designed to teach basic skills and to increase awareness of teammates. Like our coach, your child's coach might even have the players practicing to music!

# PART III:
# YOU AND
# YOUR CHILD

**Fig. 7.1** Dozens of soccer players dribble merrily through the wooded grounds of the campus where they are attending a soccer school. Photo used by permission of Puma All-Star Soccer School.

# Skill-Building Games to Play With Children

A variety of simple exercises and games will increase your child's skill and give both of you hours of pleasure. Whatever you do together, your main goal should be to have a good time and enjoy each other's company. If, in the process, your child's skills (and maybe even yours!) improve, that's a bonus. I'll repeat my caution that soccer is highly contagious. More than one parent has ended up coaching, taking referee's training, finding an adult team to play for, or all three.

Paul Harris suggests judging any practice game or drill by two criteria: Does it help players to build skill or develop their bodies? Can they get a feeling of success from what they are doing? The answer should be "Yes" on both counts.

In South America the most popular ball, and most children's first ball, is a ragball. It won't bounce, so it can't easily get away from a child, and it rolls unpredictably, so it gives children a chance to learn how to control it. And because it is very light, it makes an ideal first ball for heading practice. To make a cheap ragball easily, simply collect ruined stockings and panty hose. Stuff them into the toe of one stocking. When the toe is well stuffed, stitch the stocking just above where the stuffing ends and cut off the rest. You can use this ball with any child, no matter what age. Using it helps children learn how to feel the ball with the foot almost as well as they can with the hand.

## Opening Moves

For fun, fitness, and prevention of injury, consider starting any practice session with some conditioning exercises. With a little imagination, you'll be able to adapt many common exercises to a version that involves a soccer ball. For instance, you can do sit-ups together with your hands over your head, holding a soccer ball. Or, try leg lifts with a ball held between the ankles.

## Games for Very Young Children

If your child is five or younger, your main goals should be to have fun and to help the child become accustomed to the ball. Fecht suggests that the parent and child try sitting facing each other with legs spread wide like two "Vs." Then roll the ball gently back and forth.

If you try kicking exercises, keep them simple. Don't worry about accuracy. Some authorities suggest concentrating on helping the child learn to kick with the inside of the foot. Start by letting him or her kick a stationary ball, which you retrieve. As skill builds, you might want to begin rolling the ball slowly for a short distance to give practice with a moving ball. Also let the child practice kicking barefoot (see Figure 7.1). Bare feet feel the ball better and discourage kicking with the toe.

Other authorities feel that preschoolers are too young to concentrate on specific skills. They recommend showing children pictures of proper technique, which they can imitate if they wish, watching soccer games together on television, and encouraging play with a tennis ball, a ragball, or a light volleyball rather than a soccer ball.

If you try heading exercises, use a ragball. A smack in the face from a harder ball is enough to discourage a child from heading for some time. Furthermore, very young children don't have the strong neck muscles needed to head a heavier ball. You might start by bouncing the ball gently against your own forehead to give the child the idea. Keep your eyes open and your mouth shut. When your child is ready to try this, tell him or her to keep eyes open and mouth shut, too. Then, keeping the ball in your hands, touch it gently to his or her forehead at the hairline several times. Gradually work up to short, gentle passes in which the ball is gently tossed from your hand.

If you have several children, older ones may also want to help. Supervise to make sure the help is properly given, and don't let an older child practice heading with a younger one until you are sure the passes will be gently given.

# Games and Exercises for Older Children

Older children not only enjoy working out with you; many also want some equipment for working out by themselves. When your child reaches that point, consider getting a pendulum ball or tether net. Hitched to the ankle, the ball can be kicked and easily retrieved. Hung from a tree limb or garage beam (check height carefully), it becomes a useful tool for heading practice. For a picture of a pendulum ball, see Figure 4.4, Part B.

### Trapping

Trapping — ball control — is a hard skill to master. With children nine years old or younger, practice with a ragball. With older children, use a soccer ball. Toss the ball gently to the spot on the body where your child is trying to learn to trap. For instance, if your child is learning the leg trap, throw the ball gently at about calf height. Practice the drill until he or she can catch the ball with that part of the body, drop it to the ground between the legs, and begin dribbling it. When one type of trap has been mastered, practice another.

### Kicking

When you practice kicking, use both feet and encourage your child to do the same. Practice kicking with the inside and the outside of the foot, avoiding the toe. As the child's skill and accuracy grow, gradually increase the distance between the two of you, and the child's accurate kicking range will gradually increase. Also try kicking back and forth barefooted in sand or grass.

For shooting practice, set two cones, flags, or boxes in the positions of goal posts (8 yards apart) and let your child practice kicking from 12 yards away, which is the distance between the penalty spot and the goal posts. As the child's skill grows, encourage shots from farther and farther away and at different angles. Be sure to encourage shots with both feet.

You can also encourage target practice by having the child practice shooting at a can or cone in the yard.

**Fig. 7.2** This player's face reflects the total concentration that all good soccer players learn. Photo used by permission of Puma All-Star Soccer School.

## Passing

Passing teaches children how to control the direction of the ball. Practice short passes first, long ones later. Start at one edge of your yard. Both of you will move forward, slowly at first. Whoever has the ball passes it to the other, forward and at an angle, so that the ball arrives as the receiver gets to the spot. The receiver then passes the ball back, again in a forward direction. This teaches "lead passing." The pattern looks like this (the solid lines represent the path of the ball; the broken lines represent the path of the players). Note that the two players form two points of a triangle. The spot where ball and player meet is the third point. Repeat the pattern slowly, then pick up speed as skill improves. Later, you may want to add "two-touch" or "three-touch" dribbling between passes. For example, in two-touch dribbling, the player can only touch the ball twice before passing off.

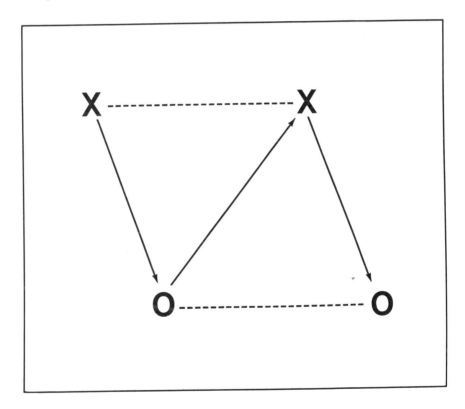

## Heading

See the instructions on heading in the section on very young children. With children over nine, practice with a soccer ball. If you own a volleyball net, set it up in the back yard and encourage your child to play soccer volleyball (socleyball) with friends to develop heading skills.

**Fig. 7.3** Here players improve their heading skills by playing "socleyball," a version of volleyball.

**Fig. 7.4** On the facing page, players are practicing dribbling through cones. Players can make their own practice course at home with coffee cans filled with sand, cardboard boxes, or any other object that stands off the ground and won't blow around in the wind. Photos used by permission of Puma All-Star Soccer School.

## Dribbling

Dribbling and kicking barefooted is as good for older children as for younger ones. Another good exercise is to set up a slalom-like obstacle course in the yard. As obstacles, use trees, bushes, cones, bicycle flags stuck in the ground, boxes, or anything else you can think of. Plan the course so the obstacles are three or four feet apart. The child dribbles in and out around the obstacles like the players in Figure 7.4.

With a child twelve or older, time the run. Write the date and time in a pocket notebook. As time passes, you'll both have the pleasure of seeing improvement in the form of steadily declining times. If you leave the course set up, the child can practice when you're not around.

Variations: 1) dribbling with just the weak foot (usually the left), using both the inside and the outside of the foot to keep the ball going; 2) using tall markers, such as trees or bicycle flags, to encourage keeping the head up and eyes forward, which is necessary in a game if a player is to find teammates to pass to; 3) dribbling with the sole of the foot, pushing it forward with the bottom of the foot and pulling it back with the toes; 4) as dribbling skill builds, having the child add fakes. Dribbling, as with all soccer moves, has its own rhythm. Fakes simply alter the rhythm.

A variation on 2) is to have the child dribble in the open yard, with you pointing the direction in which to go and changing the direction every 10 or 15 seconds. This exercise has two benefits. It increases dribbling flexibility and encourages children to keep their heads up. (If they don't, they can't tell where to go.)

## Juggling

Juggling, the skill of bouncing the ball off the feet, thighs, shoulders, head, etc. (any place except hands and arms), helps players to warm up and encourages familiarity with the ball. Lowell Dickmeyer occasionally offered his son a small reward for a certain number of juggles without stopping. He always set the limit a bit higher than he knew the child could reach at that time, so he'd have something for which to shoot. Dickmeyer reports that the offer was too successful. Every time he sat down to read, his son wanted him to come watch because he was certain he could reach the specified number.

## Goalkeeping

Goalkeepers need to develop skill at reaching and diving for balls. If your child has decided that goalkeeping is for him or her, talk with the coach about helpful exercises and ask for demonstrations with your child.

## Rainy Days

For rainy days, Paul Harris recommends a board game, Subbuteo, that, he claims, is "soccer's answer to Monopoly." It is available from Subbuteo, Jokari/US, Inc., 4715 McEwen Road, Dallas, Texas 75234.

**Fig. 8.1** Four Indiana players pose happily after a game with the trophy their team has just won. Photo used by permission of Indiana University Women's Soccer Club.

# Soccer and Your Child's Health

In soccer, as in any other sport, your child's mental and physical good health can be nurtured only by the cooperative efforts of all parties involved.

Children benefit from sports generally by achieving mental, emotional, and physical goals. Soccer is especially beneficial because it helps children develop physical endurance, agility, and cardiovascular fitness. In fact, Galton considers it one of two "best buys" in sports. Furthermore, at least until puberty, there's no reason why boys and girls can't play on the same teams. Even after puberty, though, many women play successfully on recreational teams with men because soccer depends more on intelligence and skill than on size.

## Mental Health

Children benefit mentally from sports when they can play without pressure from win-at-any-cost coaches and parents. It's wise, then, for parents to get to know the coach's philosophy and watch a few practices and games to find out how he or she handles children under pressure.

It's also most important to examine your own attitude as a parent. If your goals for your child's participation in sports are more important to you than your child's goals, your child will suffer. If you are trying to achieve your own dreams of glory through your children, they will suffer. They will either rebel or try too hard to please you, thereby depriving both of you of the pleasures and growth that sports can bring.

Support your child by attending as many games as possible and by helping at practice if the coach wishes. When your child does well or the team wins, rejoice. When it loses, dish out hugs and sympathy. Remember, wins and losses don't reflect on you. They are a team achievement and as such belong to your child's team as a whole.

Many parents, especially those who didn't participate in sports when they were young, are surprised at the strength of the emotions they feel when watching their children play soccer. Normally re-strained to the point of inhibition, I was shocked to find myself jump-ing up and down and cheering wildly on the sidelines. Similarly, en-thusiasm rapidly turns to anger when it appears an opponent has fouled and not been caught.

And it turns swiftly to gut-wrenching fear when your child goes down with an injury. I'll never forget the first time Rob went down in a tournament with a hard-kicked ball that caught him in the chest and (I learned later) knocked the wind out of him. I had no medical training, and all I could do was worry. I learned, eventually, that I could best help my son by remaining on the sidelines and keeping quiet. That way, he wouldn't be worried by the look on my face or the sound of my voice. Indeed, the referee may insist that the parents of an injured player stay off the field unless waved on by him or her.

Galton suggests several steps parents *can* take. Watch for any of the following signs, which may mean that your child's mental health is less than the best:

- Gaps between what the child *wants* to do and what he or she is *able* to do.
- Accident proneness.
- Fighting, blind rage, or plunging into painful situations with no apparent sense of pain.
- Exaggeration of injuries.

When these symptoms exist, the problem may be strictly within your child. However, it may also be that your child is feeling excessive pressure from either you or the coach. Examine yourself honestly, talk with the coach, and talk with your child. Listen for what's said and what isn't. Getting to the bottom of the problem is crucial if your child is to enjoy soccer.

**Fig. 8.2** This stretching chart shows players how to warm up for a game or practice. Chart reproduced by permission of John Beaulieu, Stretching Charts, P.O. Box 3288, Department P, Eugene Oregon 97403.

# Physical Health

The sections that follow are not a first-aid guide. Their purpose is solely 1) to explain common injuries and treatments and 2) to explain some common ways to prevent injuries.

### An Ounce of Prevention . . .

As Galton points out, nearly every child can participate in sports, even children with heart disease, asthma, epilepsy, skeletal deformities, or mental retardation. Nevertheless, start your child's soccer career with a physical examination by a qualified physician. Repeat the physical every year that your child plays. Keep tetanus shots up to date. Make sure that the soccer program and the coach emphasize good sportsmanship. Discuss the value of sports with your child to help develop a proper perspective.

Of particular importance, buy well-made equipment, especially shoes and shinguards, and keep it in good condition (for tips, see Chapter 3). If your child is male, insist on a youth athletic supporter to protect his genitals. Failing that, buy shorts that come with a built-in underpant, which serves the same purpose. One such short is the Adidas Mexico. Some players wear an athletic supporter with a metal cup to protect themselves. (I've found that coaches disagree on whether the metal protector is necessary or even a good piece of equipment to use.)

If your child is a girl with developing or developed breasts, get her a firm brassiere to give some protection from a hard ball to the chest.

Feed your child a sound nutritious diet. Keep a sick or injured player home from practice and games.

Proper warming up, cooling down, and general conditioning help to prevent injury. Lots of children get impatient with these steps, preferring to get right to playing. Take the time, then, to explain the benefits to your child. You may want to talk to the coach first to learn which exercises have what specific benefits. While you're at it, ask the coach to discuss warm-ups, conditioning, and cool-downs with the players. Some children will take a coach more seriously than a parent.

You might also want to buy a copy of a stretching chart (shown in Figure 8.2) to help your child learn the function of various exercises.

Our family learned the importance of warm-ups the hard way. I had gotten lost driving to a game and Rob arrived only a few minutes before the game. His warm-ups were hasty at best. Within minutes he was out with a sprained ankle that was partly due to the inadequate warm-up.

**Fig. 8.3** Players warm up before every practice and game. These players are doing an inner thigh stretch. Photo used by permission of Puma All-Star Soccer School.

Players also prevent injuries by learning how to make body contact. Our coach explains that players are more likely to get hurt if they shy away from contact than if they move actively into it. The act of moving helps to repel contact. He even holds bumping drills to help the players learn how to handle body contact. If you observe one of these drills, don't be alarmed. Your child is simply learning self-protection.

## First-Aid Supplies

At minimum, every team's first-aid kit should contain the following items. The list is in alphabetical order:
- Adhesive tape — several sizes.
- Ammonia caps for dizziness.
- Antiseptic solution.
- Aspirin.
- Bandages.
- Blankets.
- Copies of each player's medical treatment permission form.
- Cold packs and ice.
- Elastic wraps and bandages of various types and sizes.
- Eyewash solution with eyewash glass.
- Gauze pads.
- A small notebook for recording phone locations and ambulance numbers.
- Plastic bags (sandwich bags do nicely) to hold ice and cloths to wrap around the bags when they are used to ice down an injury.
- Salt or salt tablets for hot, humid weather.
- Scissors.
- Soap.
- Tongue depressors.

If you can find a doctor or nurse among the parents of your players to tend the first-aid kit and attend most practices and games, so much the better.

Tape a quarter for a phone call inside the cover of the kit along with a piece of paper that lists the telephone number of the nearest ambulance service. Find the phone that is nearest each game or practice site. Write that information on a piece of paper and tape it on the lid of the kit.

When a team plays away from home, the coach, manager, or a parent should be responsible for locating the nearest phone and ambulance service number and writing this information in the kit notebook. Teams in an association should share this information as they collect it. Then the effort will take little time from any one team.

Don't be alarmed by these precautions. This information is rarely needed. The only point I wish to make is that when it *is* needed, it will probably be needed in a hurry. Injured players' needs can be met more swiftly when parents and coaches have taken proper precautions.

Now let me tell you about the most effective cure we've found for nearly any nonserious injury. The "Magic Sponge," as it's known, is not original with our team. I was watching a tournament game in Columbia, Maryland, between a pair of Canadian Under-15 teams, when two players collided and one went down. Hard. The referee stopped the action, and the injured player's coach and manager rushed onto the field carrying an ordinary water bucket. The water sloshed over the sides as they ran.

**Fig. 8.4** The Magic Sponge has mysterious healing powers.

When they reached the player, they knelt and checked what appeared to be an injured thigh. Then they stepped back, reached into the bucket, drew out a dripping sponge, held it about six inches above the injury, and squeezed its somewhat murky elixir over the injured spot. Twice more the sponge was dipped and squeezed. Suddenly the injured player sat up, shook himself off, stood, and jogged back into position. A magic sponge! I had never seen anything like it.

Later, watching another game between two different teams, I witnessed the appearance of another bucket, complete with *its* own magic sponge. I saw the ritual repeated several more times before the end of the tourney and have now seen it elsewhere as well.

Our coach doesn't miss a trick. By the time the Pampas' next game rolled around, our team, too, had a water bucket and sponge on the sidelines. It got used, too, with the same miraculous results.

Now the bucket comes to all practices and travels to all games. Not long ago, I arrived before the end of practice — just in time to see one of Rob's teammates go down and hear another one bellow, "Get the Magic Sponge!" (No one has been able to tell me why it is the *sponge* that is magic and not the water, the bucket, or the hand that does the squeezing.) The water may be a bit dirty by the end of a game, and I wouldn't recommend using the sponge on an open wound, but for other nonserious injuries, the sponge is a most effective remedy.

### First Aid at Home

You won't need anything special at home. The usual bandages, antiseptics, and aspirin take care of most problems. Occasionally a heating pad helps. Frequently your player will need ice. I spent a lot of time getting ice cubes out of trays until a doctor of sports medicine passed on this tip:

- Buy a package of the smallest size paper cups.
- Fill ⅔ full of water and store carefully in freezer.
- When an injury needs ice, extract a cup. Peel back the paper, and your injured player is in business with no muss, no fuss, and no ice tray to refill.

### Injuries and Common Treatments

The following injuries are listed alphabetically, not by seriousness or frequency.

**Athlete's foot**, contracted in locker rooms, showers, and swimming pool walkways, shows up as scaling and itching between the toes. Perspiration makes it worse. An early infection can be treated with nonprescription fungicidal drugs such as Desenex. Advanced infections become bacterial and usually require treatment with a drying lotion and an oral antibiotic.

**Back strains** can usually be prevented with adequate warming up. When they occur, they are usually treated with ice (immediately), rest, heat (later), and sometimes massage. When any back injury comes with severe pain and numbness or weakness in the legs, send for an ambulance and wait for its trained crew to move the player.

**Blisters** on the feet often occur near the start of a season, especially when players haven't taken the time to break in new cleats properly. The usual treatment is to prick the side of the blister gently with a sterilized needle, gently press out the fluid into a sterile gauze pad, and cover with sterile gauze and a bandage.

**Broken bones** and **dislocations** are usually marked by pain, pronounced swelling, difficulty in moving, and fear and shock in the child. Fecht cautions that an injured wrist is especially likely to be a break rather than a sprain. The injury should be immobilized and iced down, and the child taken to a doctor as fast as possible.

**Bruises** treated immediately with ice usually don't turn as blue, hurt less, and heal faster. Wearing shinguards prevents many bruises from happening.

**Cuts and scrapes** often happen, which is why every player's tetanus shots should be up to date. Simple scrapes can be treated with antiseptic and bandages. Fecht lists several signs that warn of a more serious injury: 1) the joint below the injury can't be moved, 2) the area of injury is numb, 3) the wound gapes and appears to need stitches, or 4) bleeding continues despite the use of pressure. If any of these signs exists, get the child to a doctor immediately.

**Groin pulls** are common, painful injuries for soccer players. They are common because of the violent leg motion used in kicking the ball. The only way to cure the injury is to have the player stop playing totally until the pain is completely gone.

**Heat cramps**, in the arms, legs, or stomach area, are caused by heavy sweating and loss of salt. Galton advises treatment by massaging or pressing the cramped muscles and giving the victim salt water to drink (½ teaspoon of salt to a glass of water). The victim drinks a glass of the water every fifteen minutes or so for an hour or until the cramps go away. Although very painful, heat cramps aren't considered dangerous.

**Heat exhaustion** (collapse, prostration) can occur during games played in hot, humid weather. Galton identifies symptoms as damp, cold, pale skin, heavy sweating, listlessness, fast and weak pulse, rapid and shallow breathing, and sometime semiconsciousness or unconsciousness. Preliminary signals include weakness, dizziness, nausea, headache, mild muscle cramps, and blurring or dimming vision. The usual treatment is to have the victim lie down, preferably in a cool place, with wet, cold cloths on the forehead and neck. Salt water (see "heat cramps") is also helpful. Heat exhaustion usually goes away quickly. If collapse occurs, though, get medical help fast.

June in southern Indiana (state tournament time) usually features very humid days with temperatures above 90 degrees. To combat the heat, we routinely keep wet wash rags in plastic bags in the ice chest. We recommend this quick cooler to other teams that play in hot climates.

**Heat stroke** (sunstroke) is a serious medical emergency. It occurs when the body loses its ability to regulate heat. Galton lists the symptoms as hot, dry, flushed skin, fever (often 105 degrees or higher), pulse of 160 beats a minute or more, rapid and deep breathing, pupils contracting and then dilating, muscle twitching, cramps, convulsions, and/or forceful vomiting. Early warning signs are headache, excessive warmth, and/or listlessness. An attack can come on suddenly with unconsciousness, convulsions, or delirium. Galton stresses the importance of getting medical care as rapidly as possible. In the meantime, do everything possible to reduce body temperature to prevent brain damage or death. Treatment usually includes undressing the victim and putting him or her in a tub of cold water; covering with cold, wet blankets; or sponging with cold water. During the cooling, massage the skin to help cooled blood return to the brain. The temperature should be brought down to 101 degrees but not below (otherwise it may fall dangerously low).

**Muscle pulls**, signaled by a sudden, sharp pain in a muscle, call for an immediate stop to activity. Rest, ice, elevation, and (sometimes) elastic bandages are common treatments. The ice and bandages are discontinued after 24 hours. Elevation is discontinued when swelling is gone. Some doctors believe that after two days or so, heat helps. Adequate warm-ups help to reduce the likelihood of muscle pulls.

**Nosebleeds** aren't usually a cause for concern unless the bleeding continues, the nose swells or otherwise changes size and shape, or the child is emotionally tense, has trouble breathing, or reports a medical history of bleeding or blood disorders (if such exists, make sure the coach knows about it). The child will normally be told to sit quietly, pinch the nostrils together, apply ice, and *not* blow the nose.

**Osgood Slatter**, a knee condition that afflicts some players in their early teens, appears to be brought on by rapid growth, not by injury. For many players, the only way to ease the pain and cure the injury is to stop sports for a period of time. Experts seem divided on whether continuing to play is harmful as well as painful or merely painful.

If a **permanent tooth is knocked out**, immediately pick it up and either put it in the child's mouth, in the socket if possible (tell him or her not to swallow the tooth!), or wrap it in gauze that has been soaked in a mild solution of salt water. Immediately take the child to a dentist. There is a period of about six hours when the tooth's tissue can survive and be reimplanted. Galton notes that if the reimplantation is done within half an hour, even the interior pulp may survive. This is why medical permission forms (Chapter 9) should list the dentist's name and telephone number as well as the doctor's.

Knocked-out teeth aren't common in soccer. I've seen only one tooth injury in six years, and many coaches report never having had one. When a tooth does get knocked out, though, knowledge of proper treatment can make the difference between restoration of the original and a false tooth.

**Shock** is present when a child's skin feels clammy and turns pale, chalky, or blue. (On a dark-skinned child, look for paleness around eyes and nails.) The child may feel weak, fatigued, or nauseated and may breathe heavily. The pulse will be rapid and the pupils dilated. Sometimes the child will be disoriented. A child in shock should be taken to a hospital as fast as possible. While waiting for transportation, the child will usually be kept lying down and covered, with feet elevated. Adults should check to make sure the breathing passages are clear.

**Specks in the eye** usually wash out with tears. If not, an adult will usually flush the eye with cold water or dab at it with a soft cloth. Sometimes an adult will hold a child with both arms pinned to encourage anger, which usually makes the child cry and wash out the speck. If your child has a history of eye problems, make sure the coach knows about it.

Thorough warm-ups can reduce the incidence of **sprained ankles**. The sprained ankle, which usually swells and turns red, is usually immobilized and treated immediately with ice to stop swelling and internal bleeding. Later, hot soaks for several days will help the injury heal. Fecht cautions that sprained ankles should always be checked with a doctor because an undertreated ankle can cause chronic disability.

**Tendonitis**, an inflamed tendon, requires stopping vigorous activity. Common treatment involves ice and aspirin. Soccer players are most likely to get tendonitis in the Achilles tendon, which links the calf muscle to the back of the heel bone. Healing usually takes a week or two. **Tendon rupture** is usually accompanied by agonizing pain, sudden violent muscle contraction, and (sometimes) a popping sound. The child should be taken immediately to a doctor. In the interim, the injury is treated with ice, compression, and elevation.

**Testicular injury** may occur as the result of a blow to the testicles. The player should be stretched out flat on his back with knees bent, feet flat on the ground, and told to breathe in through the nose and out through the mouth to help restore normal breathing. If the pain does not die down fairly quickly, he should be checked for swelling and to determine whether both testicles are visible. If swelling is present, application of ice may reduce it. If only one testicle is present, the child should be taken immediately to the emergency room. A testicle that has been pushed up into the abdomen can be permanently lost if not properly treated.

**Unconsciousness**, even brief instances, always requires checking by a doctor as soon as possible. Intermediate first aid includes checking breathing passages (giving mouth-to-mouth resuscitation, if necessary) and checking for head or neck injuries. In cases of head or neck injuries, the player should be moved only by experts who know how to prevent such injuries from turning into permanent paralysis.

After any **head injury**, even if unconsciousness doesn't result, watch the child carefully for 24 hours for any signs of sleepiness, difference in pupil size, repeated vomiting, irregular breathing, muscle weakness in arms or legs, blurred or double vision, persistent or severe headache, or drooping eyes or mouth.

When the **wind has been knocked out** of a player, use the nose-mouth breathing technique described in **testicular injury.**

## Effects of Injury on Your Child

Children who receive a serious injury, such as a broken bone, may be a bit overcautious when able to play again. Sometimes fear of playing occurs as the result of a nonserious but painful injury such as a badly kicked shin or a kick in the groin. Encourage the child to talk out the fear and lovingly encourage the return to full activity. Naturally, if the injury was a kicked shin, get shinguards to prevent future injuries.

Occasionally, other equipment can help. One of our players, kicked in the groin, finally bought a supporter with a metal cup to protect his testicles. He played in it for a time but found that it hindered his ability to move. He finally stopped using it, preferring freedom of motion to protection, and hasn't had a testicle injury since. Some parents might consider the money wasted. I don't. The metal protector allowed the player to get back into action and decide for himself whether he needed or wanted the extra protection.

Serious injury to a teammate, such as a broken bone, may also trouble your child, but such injuries are blessedly rare in soccer. One coach who read this chapter reported that in 2000 games, his players had experienced only one broken bone. I've seen only one, and that was a broken collarbone on a player who had broken the same bone several times before in other activities.

Overall, most soccer parents rejoice that their children's sport has a very low injury rate and is a sports "best buy" in the bargain.

# Support for Coaches, Officials And Teams

The following sections on "Support for Coaches" and "Support for Officials" are for every parent. The section on organization for league play is for parents of competitive soccer players and parents of players who are not in established community or school programs. The tasks listed are essential; if parents don't do them, the coach must.

## Support for Coaches

Your child's coach is nearly always a volunteer, often a parent like you. You can make coaching easier by encouraging your child to get to practice on time, attending games, and offering your help. If your child must miss a practice or game, let the coach know in advance.

Some coaches like to have parents help with skill drills during practice. Even parents who know little about soccer can be helpful assistants. For instance, some coaches like to have parents distribute and collect practice equipment, run trapping and heading drills, supervise skill-building drills, warm up the goalie, and provide first aid when needed.

Helping parents free the coach to work on more complicated drills with a few players at a time. Furthermore, helping with drills even benefits parents. My son's coach observes, "Most parents love to help their children with sports but feel helpless with soccer because they didn't play the game when they were young. Helping with practice teaches parents correct form and skills to use in workouts at home."

During games, many coaches want parents to help distribute and collect equipment, provide refreshments and water, and sometimes act as linesmen. Later sections in this chapter list more ways parents can help coaches.

When you attend a game, cheer for your child and others. Don't criticize a child's play. Your job is to support and encourage. If correction is in order, leave that to the coach. Chapter 8 tells how your attitude can affect your child.

Get to know the coach as soon as possible. You want to make sure his or her philosophy isn't to win at any cost. Such a philosophy can warp a child's view of the game and may even risk the physical health of children if the coach pressures injured stars to play despite the injury. Encourage the coach to get an assistant coach, perhaps one of the parents or a high-school age soccer player. The assistant can take over when the coach is absent. Also, 15-18 lively players is a lot for one adult to handle.

**Fig. 9.1** The coach explains a point during a break in practice. Picture used by permission of Hubert Vogelsinger, Puma All-Star Soccer School.

Most teams need administrative and managerial support, although recreational teams require much less. They also require money. Unless your team has financial sponsorship or the support of a well-established organization, you may need to charge dues to cover the expenses of equipment, travel and tournament fees (for competitive teams), office supplies and services, line paint, balls, and uniforms. If you don't have sponsorship, you and the coach will wind up paying from personal funds for everything from initial uniforms and equipment to after-game cokes for players without money. A dozen cokes won't break many of us. A dozen soccer balls is quite a different matter. Dues of $10 or $15 per season should be more than adequate for a recreational team. Competitive teams often need to charge more.

## Support for Officials

Your behavior toward officials will influence your child's attitude. If you treat officials with respect, so will your child.

You are unlikely to encounter a dishonest referee. You will, however, see many who are inexperienced. Soccer is a new enough game in America that many organizations scramble hard to train enough referees to keep up with the demand for their services. All USSF-certified referees have to pass a rigorous battery of written and physical tests before receiving their licenses, but most new referees need to work many games before the required skills become second nature. Linesmen, two of whom often work with the referee, receive the same training and should be accorded the same respect as referees. Often, inexperienced officials break in by working recreational games.

Whatever the officials' degree of experience, give them your full support. Don't question calls or shout names. It's poor sportsmanship, and you will teach your child bad habits. Furthermore, the problem may not be the referee — it may, instead, be your faulty understanding of the game. (For help understanding the rules, read Chapter 5.)

To help you understand a referee's calls, Figure 9.2 shows the various hand and arm signals and calls. These are NCAA-approved signals and may vary a bit from one area to the next.

If possible, take a refereeing course yourself. You'll appreciate the game more, and you'll gain a hobby that yields extra income. The beginning license requires about 16 hours of classroom study and passing grades on physical and written tests. Registration fees cost about $30 per person (this varies from one area to another), and a regulation uniform costs about $45. With fees ranging from a low of $6 (some recreational leagues) to $50 and more per game, though, most referees easily recover their basic costs and make a profit.

**Fig. 9.2** National Collegiate Athletic Association referees use these signals to indicate their calls. Although most of these signals are standard, the choice of signal for a few calls may vary from one sponsoring organization to the next. If you see a signal you don't understand, ask the referee about it after the game. This illustration is used by permission of the National Collegiate Athletic Association

# Organization for Competitive Play

State leagues have registration procedures, registration fees, and occasional meetings for officials. To register a team:

1. Ask the state league for registration forms. Expect to receive several cards and a roster form.
2. Pay the registration fee.
3. Complete the registration cards for each player. For each player:
   a. Get proof of birth — a copy of either a birth certificate or a passport will do. Deal directly with parents because original certificates and passports are hard to replace. Make *three* copies of the proof — two for the state and one to keep in the team's records (this simplifies reregistration in future seasons). Return the originals to the players' families.
   b. Also get two wallet-sized photographs of each player. Copies of a passport photograph will do. Two copies of snapshots are also fine. A quick solution: take a Polaroid camera to practice, group the players, take two pictures of each group, and then cut the pictures apart.
   c. Fill out the card or have parents and players fill them out. Make sure parents and players sign the cards where necessary.
   d. Clip each player's pictures to his or her card.
   e. Write a check to cover the registration fee for individual players (in our state, the cost is $1.50 per registrant, or $24 for an 18-player team). This fee is *in addition to* the team registration fee. (In Indiana, the team fee has been about $175 per season.)
   f. Mail cards and fees to the appropriate state official. Within a week or two the team's copies of the cards will be appropriately validated and returned.
4. Have the players sign the roster. Mail it to the appropriate official.
5. Find out how playing schedules are set up and when you will receive a copy. Also find out who is responsible for assigning and paying referees.
6. Make sure you get a copy of the league and other rules under which your team will be playing.

I cannot overstate the importance of the player passes. At each game the referees will check the players with their passes to ascertain that the players present are indeed the players registered. If the passes aren't there, the team can't play. If a single player's pass is missing, he or she can't play.

# Basic Communications

The passes and roster will help you set up team communication. Before mailing the forms to the league:

1. Alphabetize the passes.
2. Type an alphabetic list that shows parents' and players' names, addresses, and telephone numbers. You may also want to type a telephone "tree," in which one player, at the top, calls two teammates who, in turn, each call two more teammates, and so forth until players at the bottom of the tree have been reached. Trees speed up communication and don't put all the calling effort on one or two people.
3. Type a medical and travel information and release form. Figure 9.3 shows a typical one.
4. Duplicate and distribute the address list, telephone tree, medical form, bill for season fees, practice and game schedule, and, if desired, a letter of explanation to parents.

Communication is much simpler for teams that have a fixed practice schedule and fixed arrangements for cancellation in case of rain. Some teams hold practice rain or shine. When rain makes outdoor practice impossible, they either practice indoors in a gymnasium or talk strategy in a borrowed classroom.

Some organizations prepare regular newsletters. If yours does, mail it to the players' homes. Don't try to send the letter home from practice with the players. If you do, I guarantee the letter will get lost on the way.

# Liability & Medical Insurance

Some kinds of insurance are available from national soccer organizations. Sometimes local insurance agents will donate a year's worth of liability insurance to a team or group of teams. If you have players who are *not* covered by family medical plans, encourage them to take out one of the inexpensive student policies that are offered through many schools, usually when school starts in the fall.

It is also important that when you receive completed medical forms from your team, you duplicate them at least three times. One copy for each player goes in the first aid kit. Another copy goes in the team files, to be copied and sent, if requested, to the sponsors of the tournaments in which the team plans to play. Another copy goes in the manager's kit with the player passes. In addition, each player should carry a copy with him to all games and practices. Put the copy in an envelope and tape it to the bottom of the duffel bag most players use to carry their practice gear.

This may seem a bit overprecautious. The problem is, however, that a player on a traveling team can sometimes need medical attention at a time other than a game. At one tournament, my husband took

**NAME OF SOCCER CLUB**

Travel and Medical Permission Form

Name _____ Birth Date _____

     (Last)    (First)    (Middle)

                                              Zip _____

Address _____

       (Street)         (City)     (State)

Name of parent or guardian _____

Phone: Home _____ Work _____

Physician _____ Phone: Office _____ Home _____

Dentist _____ Phone: Office _____ Home _____

Hospital _____ Date of last tetanus booster _____

Is your child subject to convulsions or epileptic seizures? _____

Does your child have any known drug allergies? _____ If yes, please explain.

_____

History of serious accident, operation, health condition, or recent medical or

dental care _____

_____

- - - - - - - - - - - - - - - - - - - - - - - - - - - - - - - - - - - - - - -

I/We, the parents/guardians of the above-named child, who participates on the [Name of Soccer Club or team] team, assume all risks and hazards incidental to conduct of the activities and transportation to and from the activities. I/We do further release, absolve, indemnify, and hold harmless the soccer program, the organizers, sponsors, and supervisors, any and all of them. In case of injury to my/our child, I/we hereby waive any claims against the organizers, sponsors, and any supervisors appointed by them. I/We also release from responsibility anyone who transports my/our child to and from activities.

I/We also recognize that an injury requiring immediate medical attention might be sustained during practice, in a game, or while being transported to or from a game or practice. In the event of such an injury to my/our child and neither I nor my spouse can be contacted immediately, I/we do hereby grant permission to the attending physician and the hospital to render such treatment as would ordinarily be given to a patient in such condition, and I/we agree to pay the usual charges for such treatment.

Signed _____ Date _____

Signed _____ Date _____

Health insurance held from _____

Policy Number is _____ ID Number is _____

**Fig. 9.3** A completed medical and travel permission form enables emergency treatment of injured players when parents are not present. It also protects the team or sponsoring association from law suits in the event of an accident.

a player to the hospital with an injured wrist while the coach finished out the game. He used the form in the manager's kit. Later that day the swelling of a bad bruise on another player's leg disturbed his host mother, and she took him to the doctor using the medical form in his bag. On the two other occasions, in five years, when medical treatment has been needed, the parents were present, so the forms weren't needed.

# Support for Games

### Needed by Each Team for All Games

- **Player passes**, preferably in a separate envelope, clearly addressed to the team manager in case of loss.
- **Medical permission forms** and **first aid kit.**
- **Bicycle pump and inflation pin** for pumping up balls; **flatproof sealant** for mending leaks.
- **Water and ice in a cooler** for refreshment and treatment of injuries. For 18 players, in 90-degree heat or higher, plan for at least four gallons of water and two bags of ice. One bag and three gallons will do when the weather is in the low 80s or below.
- **Wash cloths soaked in ice water** to cool down hot players on very hot days. (Store the cloths in plastic bags inside the ice container.)
- Optional: **orange sections** in plastic bags.
- Optional: **lost and found** box. Players abandon an amazing amount of clothing on the field. Most parents are grateful for a chance to retrieve missing items.
- Optional: **paper and pencil** to take notes for a simple news release. Stories are great for players' morale. They also make excellent scrapbook material for fund-raising efforts.

The team's medical supplies will fit neatly into a small basket or box. Keep the medical forms and player passes in an accordion file. Keep the file, the first-aid kit, the game ball, and the pump in the manager's or coach's car.

All league games require:

- **A field** that is level, reasonably smooth, and well mowed. The younger the players, the smaller the field is likely to be. Chapter 2 describes the playing field in detail.
- **Goal posts and nets**, which can be either portable or permanent. Even when the posts are permanently installed, parents often need to put up and take down nets for each game.
- **White marble dust or white paint** and **line painter** to mark boundaries of the field, the goal box, and the center line. Never use lime, which can damage the skin and eyes of players and spectators who are hit by the ball.

- **Corner flags**, flexible poles about 6 feet tall, with red, triangular flags attached, to mark the corners and center lines. Bicycle flags work very well.
- **Linesman's flags**, which the linesmen wave when a ball goes out of bounds. Licensed referees and linesmen often carry their own set.
- **Two fully inflated game balls.**
- **Officials**, at least one licensed referee and two linesmen. The home team should contact these officials well before the game. Make sure they have directions to the playing field and are told the time the game is to start.

## Needed for Games Away from Home

Player passes, medical permissions and supplies, practice balls, water and ice, and so forth are needed as usual. In addition, a team needs:

- **Drivers and cars or a bus** to take players to and from games.
- **Players' food money** when, as often happens, the team has to have a meal on the road.
- For younger teams: **one parent designated to hold players' money.**
- A **map** that shows how to get to the soccer field.
- For nonleague tournaments:
  a. Payment of **registration fees**, which often are due in advance.
  b. **Application for travel** or **travel permit**, which is issued by a team's local league and requires advance notification of league officials. Check league rules to find out how far in advance.
  c. **Advance roster** of team players who will compete in the tournament.

## Overnight Trips

Overnight trips require all the preparations of other away games. In addition, the team needs:

- **Overnight lodging**, preferably arranged for in advance. Sometimes the host team members house ("billet") visiting team members. Apart from saving money, this practice helps players to make friends wherever they travel.
- **Additional food money.**
- **Chaperones.** The younger the team, the more additional adults a coach needs. Teams up through Under-14 age need at least two adults besides the coach. Besides chaperoning, these people give the coach adult company.

**Fig. 9.4** Contrary to appearances, flying lessons are not an essential part of soccer training. Photo used by permission of the United States Soccer Federation.

**Fig. 9.5** The 1982 Umbro Select Squad leaves for a trip to England. Picture used by permission of Umbro Soccer Education Division.

# APPENDIX A

# Soccer Organizations

This appendix briefly describes organizations that deal with soccer in the United States. I give addresses only for organizations that parents might need to write to or deal with personally. In high school and college play, communication is usually handled by school officials.

## Federation Internationale de Football Association

Founded in 1904, the Federation Internationale de Football Association (FIFA) is the official world governing body of soccer. Soccer games throughout the world follow either FIFA rules or FIFA rules with slight variations. The FIFA's address is:

Federation Internationale de Football Association
Hitziweg 11, 8030
Zurich, Switzerland

## United States Soccer Federation

Many American teams, from local through professional, are registered with the United States Soccer Federation (USSF), which is the only soccer organization in the United States that is recognized by FIFA. The USSF's address is:

United States Soccer Federation
Suite 4010
350 Fifth Avenue — Empire State Building
New York, NY 10018

# United States Youth Soccer Association

The United States Youth Soccer Association (USYSA), formed in 1974, is the Youth Division of the USSF. The USYSA is composed of state youth soccer associations, which are, in turn, composed of local youth soccer associations and leagues. The USYSA is organized on democratic principles, with its affiliated members having elected representation at all levels.

The USYSA recognizes recreational, competitive, and select-team soccer. All three kinds require the same basic resources — fields, players, coaches, balls, officials, and administrative help to keep straight who plays whom on what fields, when, and with what officials — but differ in some of their fundamental goals. USYSA benefits youth programs by providing organizational assistance (in the form of visual aids and manuals), training programs for coaches and referees (including standards for certification), and low-cost medical and liability insurance to protect players, coaches, managers, and administrators (including local recreation departments and schools).

**Fig. A.1** Who'll get there first? Members of the USA team surround an opponent. Photo used by permission of the United States Soccer Federation.

The USYSA benefits players directly by offering team competition at all levels, including recreational. The USYSA's Merit Awards Program, a non-competitive program, is designed to help players at all levels to develop basic soccer skills. The program provides motivation by offering gold, silver, and bronze patches as recognition for individual achievement. A similar program, the Score with Skills Contest, is designed to test players in a skillful and competitive way. The skills are consistent with the individual skill development of the Merit Awards Program.

The USYSA's address is:

United States Youth Soccer Association
Suite 4010
350 Fifth Avenue — Empire State Building
New York, NY 10018

# American Youth Soccer Organization

The American Youth Soccer Organization (AYSO), founded in September 1964, has grown from only nine teams in its first season (1965) to more than 15,000 teams in 1980-81. AYSO's emphasis on recreational soccer stems from two guiding principles: 1) everybody plays and 2) teams are balanced by random drawing. Like the USSF, AYSO offers training for coaches and referees and includes opportunities for youths to learn coaching and refereeing skills. As of 1981, AYSO was not affiliated with the USSF or USYSA. AYSO's address is:

American Youth Soccer Organization
5403 West 138th Street
Hawthorne, CA 90250

# Soccer Association for Youth

The Soccer Association for Youth (SAY), founded in 1967 with fewer than 200 players, had more than 50,000 players and 3,305 teams registered in 1981. SAY objectives emphasize "maximum participation with even competition at various age levels." Based in Cincinnati, Ohio, SAY has teams in Alabama, Ohio, Indiana, Kentucky, Michigan, Virginia, and Wisconsin. The address is:

SAY Soccer USA National Office
5945 Ridge Avenue
Cincinnati, OH 45213

# High School and College Soccer Associations

Until the 1970s, little soccer was played in the nation's high schools. Since then, the sport has been spreading through schools in Florida, Ohio, California, and other states. In some schools it is still played as a club (non-varsity) sport, but in others it has achieved varsity status. The governing organization is the National Federation of State High School Associations.

In the nation's colleges, soccer is becoming a popular sport for both men and women, with men and women playing together on some intramural teams. Although some soccer teams are club (non-varsity) teams, the trend is toward the establishment of varsity teams. College soccer is governed by several bodies: the National Collegiate Athletic Association (NCAA), the National Association of Intercollegiate Athletics (NAIA), the Intercollegiate Soccer Association of America (ISAA), and the National Junior College Athletic Association (NJCAA).

## APPENDIX B

# How to Start A Team And Organize Parent Support

What do you do when you and your soccer-playing child move to an area with no soccer program? In our town, nearly a third of the population moves away each year, and a new third takes its place. Because ours is a college town, the turnover rate is a bit higher than it is in other places. Nevertheless, moving is a pretty typical experience all across the United States. When you find yourself stuck in Anytown with no visible team and a youngster who is champing at the cleats, don't panic. Here are tips on starting a team and organizing parent support.

## Starting a Team

### Get Background Information

Start with a letter to the United States Soccer Federation or the American Youth Soccer Association (addresses are in Appendix A). Ask for samples of their informative booklets and pamphlets on youth soccer. They give information on training clinics, codes of conduct, organization, special programs, publicity, and so forth, and can be ordered in quantity. Also ask for information on membership and for the address of your state soccer association.

When you contact the state organization, ask for addresses of soccer organizers in your local area. Also ask for a schedule of clinics to train coaches and referees. If a local association exists in your town, talking to one of its officials probably will be the most efficient way to find a team for your child.

## Look for Players

To find teammates for your child, start by telling everyone you meet at church, parties, swimming pools, track meets, doctors' offices, classes, professional meetings, and the like. Also get in touch with local schools, the local parks and recreation department, and local youth organizations such as the Boys' Club, the Girls' Club, YMCA, and YWCA. Write public service notices for local radio stations and newspapers. Try to interest a local sports columnist in soccer and entice him or her to do an article on the sport and on the team you hope to start.

Somewhere amidst an organization or school, you might find a poorly publicized team or league already in existence. If not, write a note for the organization's newsletter or make an announcement at the next general meeting. At schools, make an announcement at a parents' meeting, and prepare a form letter to be handed out in class. It could be as simple as:

Anyone for Soccer?
We want to start a soccer team for boys and girls born in 19____ or 19____. If you are interested, call [give telephone number].
John and Jean Parent

We can virtually guarantee enough response to start a team. People who are interested in soccer will put you in touch with others, who will introduce you to still others. We never cease to be amazed at the number of closet soccer fanatics we find. Our small network of Bloomington soccer people grew rapidly to include the organizers of teams all over Indiana, Kentucky, Ohio, and Illinois.

When potential players contact you, get names, addresses, telephone numbers, and birth dates. You might also want to ask for a check to cover the cost of USSF registration. Even if you plan only local competition, registering players gives them official documentation. If you are deluged with calls, schedule an organizational meeting and ask families to bring pictures and birth certificates. (For help with registration, see the instructions in Chapter 9.)

As soon as you have 18 players, a coach, and a field, set a mutually convenient practice time. If your area has no public soccer fields, look for open space you might borrow from a church, school, or local business or realtor. The local parks board might also be willing to loan space.

## Look for Coaches and Referees

You can find coaches and referees the same way you find players. If you are lucky, you'll find at least one of each, already licensed. At worst, you'll wind up recruiting people to take the training courses. The beginning courses require an investment of about $15 and between 12 and 20 hours, often on a weekend. Try to find a coach who emphasizes skill training. Try to find referees who are fair, knowledgeable, and able to control a game. Players risk injury when a referee lets rough play go unchecked.

# Organizing Parent Support

In general, the younger the team, the more necessary is parent support. For recreational teams support is often informal. In contrast, competitive teams often need formally organized support for transportation, managing, fund-raising, occasional parties, and so forth. As teams grow older, the players can take on driving and managing, but the process is a gradual one, and it works better if parents have established and tested procedures in advance.

### Officers

An organization's membership should include all parents whose children are playing or want to play soccer. Officers and duties are as follows:

- **President**; administration of organization, preparation of agendas, running meetings, backstop for manager.
- **Vice-President**; registration of players; relations with leagues and associations; initial collection of pictures, birth certificates, and health forms; supervision of used cleat exchange; collection of maps to out-of-town soccer fields.
- **Secretary**; preparation of minutes of all meetings; preparation and reproduction of medical forms, telephone trees, newsletters, and letters; coordination of mailings to parents; maintenance of organization's files of minutes, mailing lists, birth certificates, press clippings, maps, and so forth.
- **Treasurer**; administration of funds, keeping of proper books, preparation of bills.
- **Manager**; management of nets, fields, and equipment; scheduling of games; arrangements for trips and water and ice for games; responsible for getting health forms, registration cards, and first aid kit to all games. Large organizations often divide these tasks: a field supervisor manages all fields and associated equipment; a scheduler schedules games for all teams. Each competitive team has its own manager (recreational teams usually don't need a manager unless they have to maintain their own fields).
- **Publicity manager/fund raiser**; writing and delivering news stories on games to local radio and newspapers; management of search for sponsors and funds. In large organizations, these tasks are split, but the responsible parents need to work together on tasks such as brochures and programs for use in fund-raising.

## Meetings

The entire organization usually needs to meet once per season, usually just before it begins. Many organizations hold a second meeting at the end of the season, sometimes combined with a pot-luck dinner, for the purpose of fellowship and award-giving.

The board of officers, especially in a larger organization, usually meets monthly. The meeting should be at a fixed time (such as the first Monday evening of each month) and for a fixed length of time (1½ hours is the maximum). The organization as a whole will run more smoothly if there are guidelines for actions taken between meetings of the whole organization. For instance, the board of officers in a small organization might be empowered to make any expenditure up to $100. An amount beyond that would require either a parents' meeting or a telephone poll of parents.

Tasks will be shared more equally if the officers keep a watchful eye for tasks that could be farmed out to a single individual. Examples: finding drivers to out-of-town games; arranging for water and ice; caring for nets, corner flags, and field equipment; managing used cleat exchange; arranging for the hosting of visiting teams.

## Expansion

Parents' organizations often start around a single team. As more and more youngsters decide they want to play soccer, existing organizations can expand by either 1) forming a parents' group for each team or 2) becoming an umbrella organization to serve all teams. Parents usually prefer to take the latter course because the larger organization manages resources more efficiently, can negotiate better prices on items purchased in bulk (such as uniforms and balls), and has more fund-raising clout.

## Money

There are several ways to fund soccer expenses. Among these are:

- Activities such as selling tickets for benefit games, washing cars, and having bake sales or garage sales.
- Selling advertisements in a team program distributed at each game.
- Seeking donations of money and goods such as balls and liability insurance coverage.
- Seeking sponsorship of one or more players or teams by business, industry, or professionals such as doctors and lawyers.
- Charging dues.

## APPENDIX C

# Where to Get More Information

## Bibliography

**Books**

If you have trouble finding a book you want in your local book stores, you might want to try Soccer Books, 1365 Kowell Lane, Santa Rosa, CA, 95401.

Butterfield, S.M. *The Wonderful World of Soccer*. Santa Monica, CA: Goodyear. 1978.
   Butterfield's book, written for children of elementary school age, describes techniques and provides a fold-out field with cardboard players with which children can experiment.

Carlson, Jean. *Enjoying Soccer*. Seattle: Madrona Publishers, Inc. 1976.
   This well-written book will delight anyone who wants to know more about soccer. Carlson goes into great detail on strategy, tactics, and what happens in a game.

Chyzowych, Walter. *The Official Soccer Book of the United States Soccer Federation*. New York: Rand McNally. 1978.
   This book, by the former coach of the U.S. National Team, discusses all aspects of soccer. It is intended for coaches, teachers, students, players, and anyone else who enjoys soccer.

Clues, Andrew. *Soccer for Players and Coaches.* Englewood Cliffs, N.J.: Prentice-Hall. 1980.
  This book will help parents and players who want to know more about how to execute various soccer skills. The book is generously illustrated.

Csanadi, Arpad. *Soccer.* Budapest; distributed by Soccer Associates, New Rochelle, New York. 1965.
  Some coaches consider Csanadi's book the best available source of help in training and coaching. Others consider it outdated.

Dickmeyer, Lowell. *Coaching Very Young Soccer Players: A Handbook for Coaches and Parents.* Tacoma: ITI Soccer, Inc. 1976.
  Dickmeyer's slim book is packed with games, drills, exercises, and ideas on how to make soccer enjoyable for children aged 5-10.

Fecht, Gerald R. *The Complete Parents' Guide to Soccer.* Santa Monica, CA; Goodyear Publishing Company, Inc. 1979.
  Fecht's book, heavily biased toward AYSO soccer, will interest parents who want to know about the history of soccer.

Federation Internationale de Football Association. *Laws of the Game and Universal Guide for Referees.* English Edition with USSF supplement. 1982.
  This book lists the rules of soccer. It includes a supplement on USSF rules.

Galton, Lawrence. *Your Child in Sports: A Complete Guide.* New York: Franklin Watts. 1980.
  Galton's book will interest parents who want to explore the benefits of sports for children or who want to know more about sports medicine. Parents of handicapped children will appreciate his thorough discussion of the limits various handicaps place on participation in sports. The limits are fewer than many parents think.

Harris, Paul E., Jr. *So You'd Like to Know More about Soccer!* Manhattan Beach, CA: Soccer for Americans. 1974.
  This well-illustrated book, which can be read in two hours or less, briefly explains skills and discusses topics such as high school soccer, relationships with coaches and referees, and soccer for girls. A photo essay on Pele and a section on Kyle Rote, Jr., top off the book.

Harris, Paul E., Jr., and Harris, Larry. *Fair or Foul?* Manhattan Beach, CA: Soccer for Americans. 1978.
>    Harris and Harris provide a thorough guide to soccer officiating in the United States. Parents who want to coach or referee will find this book useful.

Kovalakides, N. *Officials Manual: Soccer.* West Point, N.Y.: Leisure Press. 1978.
>    Kovalakides' book contains the rules of soccer and explains how to be a good referee. He covers attitude and philosophy; pre- and postgame responsibilities; relationship with players, coaches, and spectators; working with other officials; and mechanics of signaling calls.

Laitin, Ken; Laitin, Steve; and Laitin, Lindy. *The World's #1 Best Selling Soccer Book.* Manhattan Beach, CA: Soccer for Americans. 1979.
>    This delightfully illustrated book was written by two teenagers and their sister for other young players. Any child will find the book both useful and instructive.

Lebow, Jared. *All about Soccer.* New York: Newsweek Books. 1978.
>    This overview places great emphasis on international soccer.

Morris, Desmond. *The Soccer Tribe.* London: Jonathan Cape. 1981.
>    This lavishly illustrated book is worth every penny ($30 worth of them) to the dedicated soccer fan. Written as an analysis of a newly discovered native tribe, Morris vividly describes rituals, ceremonies, taboos, superstitions, and beliefs. The illustrations alone make the book worth buying.

Rosenthal, Gary. *Everybody's Soccer Book.* New York: Scribners. 1981.
>    This book contains history and advice on soccer.

Ruege, Klaus. *Inside Soccer for Beginners.* Chicago: Henry Regnery. 1976.
>    This very complete book features good writing and clear diagrams.

Soccer Association for Youth. *Soccer Youth League.* Rev. ed., coach's edition. North Palm Beach, Florida: The Athletic Institute. 1981.
>    This lavishly illustrated book illustrates soccer skills in detail. Most skills are illustrated in panels of at least six pictures and often more, to show starting position, action, and follow-through.

Tutko, Thomas, and Bruns, William. *Winning is Everything and Other American Myths.* New York: MacMillan. 1976.
> This general sports book is a good antidote to win-at-any-cost thinking.

Vogelsinger, Hubert. *The Challenge of Soccer, A Handbook of Skills, Techniques and Strategy.* La Jolla, CA: Inswinger. 1982.
> This well-written book provides a wealth of information on all aspects of soccer. One chapter is devoted to community youth soccer programs.

Wolpa, Mark E., M.D. *The Sports Medicine Guide.* 2nd edition. West Point: Leisure Press. 1983
> This book describes common athletic injuries and tells how to prevent them. The book is well illustrated and contains a helpful glossary of medical terms.

Woosnam, Phil, and Gardner, Paul. *Sports Illustrated Soccer.* Philadelphia: J.B. Lippincott and Company. 1972.
> Young players will like this short paperback on skills.

**Magazines and Guides**

The addresses below are as of 1982. Stiff competition for readers has forced some excellent soccer magazines to cease publication.

*Official Scholastic Soccer Guide,* published annually by the NCAA Publishing Service, P.O. Box 1906, Shawnee Mission, Kansas, 66222, lists rule changes, statistics, records, honors, and the like in college soccer. Parents of college soccer players will find this inexpensive publication useful.

*Soccer America,* P.O. Box 23704, Oakland, CA 94623, is a national soccer weekly that keeps readers up to date with news and special features. It reports on all levels of soccer from youth through professional soccer. Makers of soccer equipment and directors of soccer camps regularly advertise in it.

*Soccer Digest,* P.O. Box 10170, Des Moines, Iowa 50340, is a monthly news digest.

*Soccer Goalpost,* Box 3651, Baltimore, MD 21214.

*Soccer Illustrated,* P.O. Box 355, Garden Grove, CA 92603, was expected to publish its first issue late in 1982.

*Soccer Monthly,* 4010 Empire State Building, New York, N.Y. 10018, is the official publication of the United States Soccer Federation.

*Soccer Now,* 5403 West 138th Street, Hawthorne, CA 90250, a quar-
terly magazine, is the official magazine of the AYSO. As such, its
emphasis is on youth soccer.

*Soccer Rule Book,* 400 Leslie Street, Box 98, Elgin, Illinois 60120, published annually by the National Federation of State High School
Associations, will interest parents whose children play high
school soccer.

# Camps and Clinics

Soccer camps and clinics abound. All provide a chance for
players to learn more about the game. Some also offer courses in
refereeing and coaching that parents can take while their children are
improving their skills.

Most of the professional soccer teams, such as the New York
Cosmos, Tampa Bay Rowdies, and Chicago Sting, run summer
camps, as do some college and university coaches. All camps have a
general program where players get instruction in all aspects of the
sport, and many offer day camp as well as residential programs.

Some camps also have a special emphasis. For instance, Joe
Maschnik's #1 goalie camp is a highly regarded school for goalkeepers. Lincoln Phillips runs one week of his camp especially for
goalkeepers, as do many other camps. And some camps — among
them Hubert Vogelsinger's, Phillips', and Umbro's — devote one or
more weeks to an intensive camp for highly talented players.

On occasion, a non-soccer camp may be useful to your child.
Our goalkeeper spent two weeks at Dr. James Brown's Indiana
University summer gymnastics camp working on jumping, body
strength, and flexibility.

On the following pages is a partial list of soccer camps across
the country. Many of the addresses were taken from advertisements
in *Soccer America.* The rest came from brochures I've picked up at
tournaments. The order is alphabetical. I include telephone numbers
if they were given. We have had personal experience with Jerry
Yeagley's Indiana University Summer Soccer Camp and Lincoln
Phillips' Soccer School and have been well pleased with both. Pictures taken at Hubert Vogelsinger's camps are scattered throughout
this book.

The pictures in Figure C.1, taken at one of Vogelsinger's camps,
show that the soccer ball sometimes takes a back seat to other activities.

Eugene Chyzowych
All-American Soccer Camp and School
61 White Oak Drive
South Orange, NJ 07079
(201) 762-5331


Eagles Soccer School Ltd.
P.O. Box 355
Garden Grove, CA 92642
(213) 436-3482


Eastern Soccer Academy — The Family Camp
Dave Johnson/Ray Franklin
2158 Allan Avenue
Yorktown Heights, NY 10598
(914) 245-6205, 528-7942


Exper/Sport, Inc./Soccer Corner Tours
P.O. Box 9038
Van Nuys, CA 91407
(800) 423-2427


Pele Soccer Camp
Soccer Camps of America
75 Rockefeller Plaza
New York, N.Y. 10019


Lincoln Phillips
Lincoln Phillips Soccer School
P.O. Box 312
Simpsonville, MD 21150
(301) 991-7591


John Rennie, Duke Soccer Camp
Cameron Indoor Stadium
Duke University
Durham, NC 27706
(919) 684-2120, 493-1325

**Fig. C.1-A** Mealtime at a soccer camp. Picture used by permission of Puma All-Star Soccer School.

**Fig. C.1-B** Coach checks camper's knee protector. Picture by S. Frinzi; used by permission of Hubert Vogelsinger, Puma All-Star Soccer School.

Cliff Stevenson, Soccer Coach
United States Soccer Camp
Brown University
Providence, RI 02912
(401) 863-2349, 434-2657

Ed Tock, Director
Tock-Easteadt Total Soccer Camp
8 John Avenue
Elmont, N.Y. 11003
(516) 328-3098

Umbro Soccer Education Division
Andrew Warner, Program Coordinator
25 East Court Street
Greenville, SC 29601
(803) 233-0000

Hubert Vogelsinger, Director
Vogelsinger Soccer Academy, c/o Puma Soccer School
5556 Ladybird
La Jolla, CA 92037
(714) 459-8475

Jerry Yeagley, Coach
Indiana University Summer Soccer Camp
Assembly Hall, Indiana University
Bloomington, IN 47405
(812) 337-0051

**Fig. C.1-C** Campers take time out for a swim. Picture used by permission of Hubert Vogelsinger, Puma All-Star Soccer School.

# Carolyn J. Mullins

is a writer, consultant, and soccer parent and is currently a Visiting Associate Professor at Virginia Polytechnic Institute and State University, jointly appointed in the English Department and the Computing Center. She has written *A Guide to Writing and Publishing in the Social and Behavioral Sciences* (Wiley-Interscience 1977), *The Complete Writing Guide to Preparing Reports, Proposals, Memos, etc.* (Prentice-Hall, 1980), *The Complete Manuscript Preparation Style Guide* (Prentice-Hall, 1982), *The Office Automation Primer* (Prentice-Hall, 1982; the last coauthored with Thomas W. West), and articles on soccer and other topics.

In 1977 her son Rob learned soccer when he joined a neighborhood team. By 1978 he was playing left halfback for an Under-12 competitive team, the Bloomington Boys Club Juniors. By 1979 the Juniors had become the Under-14 Pampas, and Carolyn and her husband, Nick, had become the Pampas' managers. Now Rob is playing Under-19 soccer, and his mother has long since lost count of the number of games she's watched, trips chaperoned, birth certificates collected, afternoon phone calls answered ("Is there practice today, Mrs. Mullins?"), and other small chores associated with managing a team.

She has gained, in return, a deep appreciation for the beauty of soccer and gratitude for a team sport that can be played by any person of any size or sex.

Along the way, soccer has ensnared all the Mullinses. Nick, son Nick, and Rob are licensed referees. Daughter Nancy plays recreational soccer as does husband Nick.

Carolyn, who watches and writes, knew nothing about soccer when Rob first started playing. She wrote this book because many parents start out just where she did—with a child who has fallen in love with a game they know nothing about. In this book are the answers she needed six years ago—a wealth of information about every aspect of youth soccer. Every chapter of the book has one major purpose: to help parents enjoy soccer as much as their children do.